HAWKER HURRICANE

Superb photograph of Hurricane Mk IIC with four cannon wing. Upper surfaces scheme shows the irregular scheme of dark earth and dark green. Yellow stripe along outer wing sections leading edges. Note also sky ring around rear fuselage.

Classic WWII Aviation

HAWKER HURRICANE

General Editor
Edward Shacklady

TEMPUS

First published 2000

PUBLISHED IN THE UNITED KINGDOM BY:

Tempus Publishing Ltd
The Mill, Brimscombe Port
Stroud, Gloucestershire GL5 2QG

PUBLISHED IN THE UNITED STATES OF AMERICA BY:

Arcadia Publishing Inc.
A division of Tempus Publishing Inc.
2 Cumberland Street
Charleston, SC 29401
1-888-313-2665

Tempus books are available in France, Germany and Belgium
from the following addresses:

Tempus Publishing Group	Tempus Publishing Group	Tempus Publishing Group
21 Avenue de la République	Gustav-Adolf-Straße 3	Place de L'Alma 4/5
37300 Joué-lès-Tours	99084 Erfurt	1200 Brussels
FRANCE	GERMANY	BELGIUM

British Library Cataloguing in Publication Data.
A catalogue record for this book is available from the British Library.

ISBN 0 7524 2000 3

Typesetting and origination by Tempus Publishing.
PRINTED AND BOUND IN GREAT BRITAIN

Contents

Series Introduction

Many different types of aircraft were involved in the Second World War, new, old, conventional, and some, downright bizarre. Any selection in a series of 'classic' aircraft will, therefore, always be arbitrary and subject to the views of individuals. The selection of aircraft for this series has been primarily governed by their operational importance, although some types have, by necessity, other claims for inclusion. The series also seeks to cover a wide spectrum of the different operations involved during the conflict as well as those countries that had a leading role.

The major powers, during the 1930s, were becoming increasingly aware that the political instability throughout the world would inevitably lead to military conflict. Many of these countries had learnt lessons from the almost haphazard preparations of the First World War and were determined not to be in that position again. During this decade, particularly the middle and the late period, there was considerable activity for the manufacturers of aircraft as it was perceived that land battles would be of less significance as the fight, using heavily armed bombers, could be taken to the very doorstep of the enemy. Most countries looked on the development and production of aircraft as a defence measure, while others realised that a strong airforce would give them a total advantage over territorial claims – whether legitimate or otherwise. The advent of Adolf Hitler's rise to power in Germany, and the increasing strength of the new *Luftwaffe*, led many nations to the realisation that to rely on their air forces' existing capabilities would be extremely unwise and that they had to expand and re-equip with more modern combat aircraft. However, despite this obvious threat no country, at the outbreak of the Second World War, had the numerical strength or modern equipment to compare with that of the *Luftwaffe*.

The Spanish Civil War (1936-1939) afforded several of the major air powers, particularly Germany and Italy, an ideal opportunity to put their newly designed aircraft to the test under battle conditions. The pilots of Germany's *Legion Condor* and Italy's *Aviazione Legionaria* evolved a number of strategies that were utilised in the early part of the Second World War and the senior officers of the *Luftwaffe* were quick to realise the need for specialised ground-attack aircraft. On the other hand, the often inferior opposition and the ease with which they were eliminated, gave the German and Italian aircrew, as well as the officials of their respective air forces, an over-estimated view of the superiority of their aircraft.

The German Messerschmitt Bf109 had been conceived in the flush of Hitler's take-over of power in 1933, and as a monoplane had complete superiority in the air until the appearance of the Spitfire. Yet the Bf109E, the 'Emil', which provided the main fighter force for Germany during the first year of the Second World War, including the Battle of Britain period, had not evolved significantly from the Me Bf109C which was the predominant fighter aircraft used by the *Luftwaffe* in the Spanish Civil War.

Italy's pilots had a totally different concept and still preferred the open cockpit and light armoury in the belief that it would enable them to out-manoeuvre their opponents.

During the immediate pre-war years the peacetime expansion of the Royal Air Force, by comparison with Germany, was slow and hampered by financial restraints. Like Italy, Britain was reluctant to dispense with their bi-plane fighters until the monoplane had proved itself. Although the manufacturers of Britain's two monoplane developments, the Hurricane and the Spitfire, were given substantial pre-war orders the RAF, by the outbreak of the Second World War, had little more than 300 Hurricanes in first-line service and approximately 150 Spitfires – less than a tenth of those ordered. In 1938, when war was very much in the offing, the RAF's weakness was only too apparent and a delegation, the British Purchasing Mission, went to the United States to order substantial quantities of US combat aircraft in an attempt to fill the gap. Most of these aircraft were not delivered until sometime in 1940 and, when war broke out, the RAF had to supplement their inferior numbers of Hurricanes and Spitfires with Gloster Gladiators and Fairey Battles which were no match for the 'Emil'.

The Soviet Union, who had also sent aircraft and pilots to the Spanish Civil War, was, in common with Britain, France and other European nations, still in the early stages of its modernisation programme. Although at the time of the German invasion the Soviet airforce was numerically strong its front-line aircraft were anything but modern. Like Britain, a few years previously, the Soviet Union had to rely on aircraft from the United States until they were able to produce, in sufficient quantities, their own.

Like the Italian pilots the aircrew of the Japanese airforce seemed to have a predilection for open cockpits and lightly armed but highly manoeuvrable aircraft. However, they discarded the bi-plane somewhat earlier and, at the time they opened hostilities against the United States, all principal first-line Army and Navy fighters were monoplanes, including the Mitsubishi Zero-Sen single-seater of the Japanese Naval Air Force.

At the time of Pearl Harbor, in December 1941, the United States' aviation industry was already producing large numbers of aircraft from orders placed on them by Britain, France and other countries. The already huge work load on the US aircraft industry was increased still further by the demand for production of behalf of its own forces. Nearly one-third of the entire US aircraft production was devoted to the manufacture of transport aircraft, with a high percentage of the remaining capacity involved with producing medium and heavy bombers. Nonetheless the overall output, from 1941 to 1945, included in excess of 12,000 Mustangs, 12,000 Corsairs, 15,000 Thunderbolts and 20,000 Hellcats and Wildcats, in addition to lesser quantities of other fighters.

The Classic Second World War Aircraft series is designed to give the aviation enthusiast a comprehensive history of many of the aircraft used during this period. Each title will cover the prototype development, production and operational use of the aircraft used by the airforces of Germany, the United States, Britain, France, Italy, Japan, the Soviet Union, and other countries that were involved in the conflict. The series will cover fighter aircraft and both heavy and medium bombers in narrative text, many black & white photographs and line drawings, and colour drawings that will show the different types of aircraft as well as the many colour schemes used by both squadrons and individuals.

Introduction

The Second World War was the greatest and most destructive conflict ever known to man. Virtually every country was to become involved, throwing into the cauldron the largest number of naval ships and merchant vessels, bombers, fighters, ground attack and reconnaissance aircraft, all for one purpose, to defeat the enemy. To operate and fight in them millions of men, and women, were engaged. It was a war that was not only fought with the armed forces on land, sea and air, but involved entire civil populations.

They, too, were subjected to bombing, invasion by foreign forces, and worked for long hours under arduous conditions to support the war effort. It was, as Hitler declared, 'Total War'. As with all wars it was to produce its heroes, villains, and legends. Of the last it was military aviation's moment to experience the same dramatic events as had been experienced with the Navy and ground forces in the First World War.

A number of these aviation legends are to be found in the monoplane fighters. Four aircraft; two British and two German, were involved in the air war from day one to final surrender of all three Axis Powers. The German fighters were the Messerschmitt Bf109 and 110 series, the design and development of which had started in the final years of peace in the 1930s. The 109 fought in virtually every great campaign in every theatre, and was continuously updated to the demands of the *Luftwaffe* from experience of the invasion of Poland; the Battle of France; Battle of Britain; the Russian campaigns and, finally, defence of the German homeland against the massive Allied bombing.

Following the war it was still in production and service, albeit not with Germany, and the numbers constructed were astronomic. Its sister aeroplane, the 110, was a long range *Zerstörer* (destroyer) and after performing badly in the Battle of Britain was developed into a first class night fighter. The British fighter to mirror the 109's history was the Spitfire. It too was born in the final years of peace and fought its way across the world. After the war many foreign Air Forces operated this great fighter, and in England it served until the jet fighter took its place.

The second great British fighter was, of course, the Hawker Hurricane and this history is devoted to examining its place in aviation history. Many legends surround it: 'Without the Hurricane the Battle of Britain would have been lost'. Certainly, that is true, but it doesn't give the whole story, as just as important was the Spitfire, without which the RAF would have had to rely upon an aeroplane design that was outdated as a pure interceptor fighter in the first year of that conflict.

The Hurricane was produced in great numbers, and developed at a slower rate than either of its two contemporaries, but was extremely adaptable despite its early airframe – a mix of wood and metal. Its shortcomings, although few in number, could be found in its early development as its designer, Sydney Camm, based the original monoplane on the superlative Fury biplane, and that can be traced back through a line of biplanes that reached back to the First World War.

CHAPTER ONE

The Doughty Warrior

From Biplane to Monoplane

The early beginnings of the Hawker Hurricane can be said to have started with the Hawker company's submission to Air Ministry Specification F.20/27 which was issued to tender during September 1927. The basic design was to undergo a complete metamorphosis over a number of years and many Air Ministry Specifications, to finally become the fighter that partnered the Spitfire in the Battle of Britain, although the designs that Hawker submitted, to the initial specification, did not resemble the later monoplane in any way

The man behind the series of designs was Sydney Camm, the Chief Engineer at Hawker Aircraft, who had developed a series of elegant fighter biplanes. These eventually evolved into two types that can be directly traced to the Hurricane, the Hawker High Speed Fury and the company's entry to Specification F.7/30, the Hawker PV3. Two further steps to the final development of the Hurricane were the Fury Monoplane and the High Speed Hurricane.

Stage Two – F.20/27 Hornet

The immediate forebear of the ultimate Fury design was exhibited, for the first time before a British public, on the Hawker-Siddeley stand at the 1929 Olympia Aero Show. It was obvious that Camm and his design team had continued the development of the F.20/27 prototype (J9123), such was its promise. However, there was a second reason for going to a revised design

In the intervening period between the appearance of J9123 and the Olympia Aero Show, Rolls-Royce had produced a new engine, the F.XIA. This engine was clearly the result of studies made of the American Curtiss Corporation's D12 unit and was a twelve-cylinder, in-line, liquid-cooled motor that allowed the building of an airframe with slimmer contours and less drag. The F.XIA produced 480hp and Camm installed a prototype in his revised F.20/27 machine.

However, this engine was also installed in the new Hawker, single-engined day bomber, the Hart, and it bestowed a speed in excess of the then current front-line RAF fighter aircraft even when fully loaded. This led to a contract for the Hawker Hart bomber.

With the failure of Specification F.20/27 to produce a replacement fighter for the RAF,

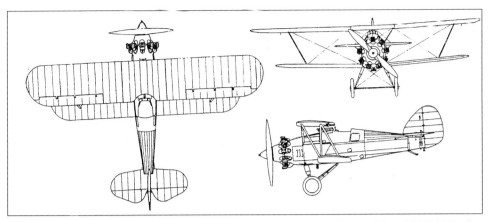

The Hawker submission to Air Ministry Specification F.20/27. It made use of the N.21/26 Hawker Hoopoe Design. Shown here with Bristol Mercury Engine.

the Air Staff cancelled it. This, however, left them with a dilemma as their front-line fighters could not intercept the newly delivered Hart bombers. After the air defence exercises of 1930 the Air Staff had to accept the reality that the only aeroplane which could successfully catch the Hart was the prototype Hawker Hornet. This aircraft had been developed as a private venture by Hawker and it was only the Martlesham Heath trials that revealed its potential.

Faced with this situation, and the inevitable delays in providing a new fighter, the

Hawker Hornet (PV). Later F.20/27 Fury Mk I (J9682), Brooklands 1929, before purchase by Air Ministry. (Hawker Aircraft)

Air Ministry purchased the prototype Hornet in September 1929 for £6,500 – a considerable sum for those days. The serial number J9682 was applied and, more significantly, the Hornet was renamed Fury to comply with Air Ministry nomenclature. Following further trials at Martlesham Heath, Air Ministry Specification 13/20 was raised and written around the design and incorporated all the desirable attributes of Hawker F.20/27 (amended in 1928) and the Hornet (Contract No. 887063/28).

Leading particulars

Aircraft configuration: Single-seat interceptor biplane fighter (experimental). *Crew:* One (pilot). *Private venture to Air Ministry Specification* F.20/27. *Engine:* One Rolls-Royce F.XIA (late F.XIS and F.XIIS), 12-cylinder, in-line, liquid-cooled of 480hp. F.XIS driving a 2-blade Watts fixed-pitch wooden propeller of 10ft 6in diameter. *Armament:* Two nose-mounted synchronised .303in machine guns. No provision for bomb carrying. *Date of first flight:* (F.XIA) 1929. *Pilot:* Flt Lt P.W.S. Bulman. *Delivery date:* Aircraft retained by Hawker for development.

Basic data

Wing span: 30ft 0in, area 250sqft. *Length:* 26ft 8.5in. *Height:* 9ft 9in. *Weights:* tare 2,338lb, gross 3,480lb. *Maximum speed:* 214mph @ 10,000ft. *Cruising speed:* 188mph. *Maximum range:* Approx 420 statute miles @ 180mph @ 10,000ft. *Rate of climb:* 2,220ft/min. *Height to time:* 10,000ft in 5min 9sec. *Service ceiling:* 27,400ft. *Number built:* One (prototype) J9682.

Fury – Fighter 'par excellence'

The decade 1930 to 1940 is of significant historical interest to the Royal Air Force as it witnessed the introduction, into Fighter Command, of two radical interceptors designed and built by two of aviation's giant Groups. Hawker Siddeley with its Hawker Fury and Supermarine with the Spitfire, both streamlined, elegant machines that served the Third Service, and British Nation during the transition from the biplane to monoplane eras.

In 1930 the first of this duo, the Fury, entered service with the RAF, and it was accepted as standard equipment in the, then, elite squadrons. Every pilot nursed ambitions to sit in the cockpit of this front line fighter, as did every schoolboy, yearning to grow up and be a Fury pilot.

The Fury was elegant, compact, fast for its time but still armed with the twin Vickers machine guns dating from the First World War. It will always be recalled as the classic biplane fighter with clean lines and shining silver cowling housing the Rolls-Royce Kestrel in-line, liquid-cooled engine which provided a maximum speed in the area of 200mph. In the late twenties, early thirties, it provided the Royal Air Force with a superb fighter. However, the Fury did not appear, magically, overnight, but was the end product of a long line of fighter development from the Sopwith Snipe of the First World War.

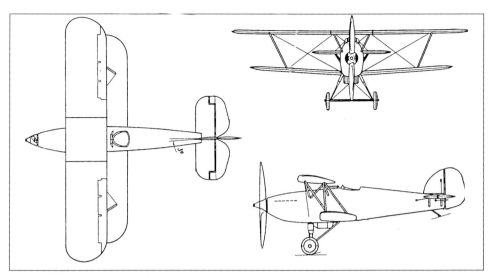

Original Hawker drawing of Fury Mk I.

In the late 1920s the Air Ministry, ever mindful of demands upon defence expenditure, issued a Specification which called for a 'fighter capable of intercepting enemy bombers that might invade British airspace'. The fighter was required to overtake, and destroy. an enemy flying at 20,000 feet at a speed of 150mph.

To reach the altitude demanded by the Specification the fighter had to demonstrate that from a standing start it could reach 20,000 feet in twelve minutes and, when there, to have a maximum speed in excess of 200mph. There was a preference for an air-cooled engine, but a liquid-cooled unit could be fitted despite the added complications of a weighty cooling system, plumbing and cooling liquids. Competitive trials made allowance for biplanes, high wing (parasol) and low wing monoplanes.

The total number of entries, biplane and monoplane, was eleven and were as follows – Armstrong Whitworth Siskin IIIA (J8627), Bristol Type 107 Bullpup (J9051), de Havilland DH77 (J9771), Fairey Firefly III (c/n F.1130), Gloster SS.18 (J9125), Hawker F.20/27 (J9123), Hawker Hornet (J9682), Saunders-Roe A10 (L2 and K1949), Vickers Type 151 Interceptor (Jockey J9122), Westland Interceptor (J9124), and Wizard (J9252), an interesting collection. An examination of these aircraft reveal how various manufacturers interpreted the specification.

Armstrong Whitworth Siskin IIA

This was a development of a line of biplane fighters based upon the Siddeley Deasy SR2 which was broadly based upon the SE series of fighters of the First World War. The prototype SR2 flew in spring 1919 and, unfortunately, had the Dragonfly engine. Three were ordered, C4541 to 43, but no production order was placed.

Little was heard of the three prototypes until March 1921 when C4541 appeared with the new Armstrong Siddeley Jaguar radial engine. The Air Ministry expressed an interest in the new configuration and encouraged the company to continue development as a PV.

The first aircraft, now called the Siskin, was the Mk II two-seat which carried the civil registration of G-EBEU and flew in the King's Cup Race of 1922. The Air Ministry accepted the revised design for Specification 14/22 by placing an order for a single prototype with the serial number of J6583 under Contract No. 342619/22, and it made its first flight as the prototype Siskin Mk III on 7 May 1923.

A series of production Contracts were placed under 19/23 to a total of 62 Mk IIIs as J6981 to 6982 (Contract No. 342619/22) with J6981/82 were registered as G-EBJQ and G-EBJS; J6998 to J7003 (Contract No. 369339/22); J7145 to J7181 (Contract No. 439840/23); J7549 to J7554 (Contract No. 53051/24); two seaters J7758 to J7764, J7820 to J7822 (Contract No. 576184/25).

Leading particulars				
Type	**SR2**	**Mk III**	**Mk IIIA**	**Mk V**
Span (ft/in)	27.6	33.1	33.2	28.4
Area (sqft)	247	293	293	256
Length (ft/in)	21.3	23.0	25.4	21.4
Height (ft)	9.9	9.9	9.8	9.4
Weight tare (lb)	1,463	1,830	2,061	N/A
gross (lb)	2,181	2,735	3,012	2,440
Max speed @ S/L (mph)	145	134	143	155
@ 15000ft (mph)	139	128	149	140
Ceiling (ft)	23,800	20,500	27,100	25,000
Climb to 20,000ft (mins)	14.0	16.5	16.9	20.2
Engine	Dragonfly	Jaguar III	Jaguar IV	Jaguar 385
Hp	320	320	385	385

J8864 to J8905 (47) to Specification 14/27, 42 Mk IIIs (Contract No. 772529/27), all built by Blackburn. J9304 to J9379 built by Bristol (27), Gloster (22) and Vickers (27). Under Specification 8/29, Contract No. 93776/29, J9872 to J9921, 50 examples of 25 August 1929 and built by Bristol (15), Contract No. 93777/29, Gloster (10) Contract No. 9377778/29. An improved variant, the Siskin IIIB was rejected. A Trainer version, the Siskin IIIDC was ordered under Contract No. Specification 1/28, Contract 823022/28, plus 32 conversions of Mk IIIs to trainers, Specification 7/28.

Bristol Type 107 Bullpup

A version of the Bulldog with 440hp Bristol Mercury IIA engine. J9051 was produced with the Jupiter VI engine under Contract No. 754492/27 and made a first flight on 28

April 1928. After trials at Martlesham Heath it was scrapped.

Leading particulars
Wing span: 30ft 0in, area 230sqft. *Length:* 23ft 6in. *Height:* 9ft 5in. *Weights:* tare 1,910lb, gross 2,850lb. *Max speed:* 190mph. *Engine/s:* 480hp Mercury IIA, 440hp Bristol Jupiter VIIF, 400hp Mercury (short stroke), 500hp Bristol Aquila.

---

de Havilland DH77

A thin, semi-cantilever winged monoplane with racers lines with the wing braced to the fuselage from upper longeron to top of main wing spar. Differential ailerons and slim 'oval' section fuselage and braced main undercarriage. One prototype J9771 to Contract 870979/38 which flew for the first time on 12 December 1929. After trials in September the aircraft was disposed of and no contract awarded. The engine, the 301hp Napier-Halford H (Rapier I) had four banks, each of four cylinders driving two crankshafts and was supercharged, and air cooled. Max speed was quoted as 200mph and landing of 60. In December 1932 it was delivered to Farnborough for trials with the Napier Rapier II engine.

Leading particulars
Wing span: 32ft 2in, area 163sqft. *Length:* 24ft 4.75in. *Height:* 8ft 0in. *Weights:* tare 1,655lb, gross 2,279lb. *Max speed:* 204mph @ 10,000ft. *Engines:* as quoted.

Fairey Firefly Mk II

Designed by Marcell Lobelle (designer of the Spitfire semi-bubble hood), the Firefly can be considered as being the fighter version of the ultra-fast Fox day bomber.

In March 1924 the company enquired of the Air Ministry for their current requirements for a single seat fighter. Acting upon the information a prototype (F.572) Firefly Mk I was designed and built and made its first flight on 9 November 1925. Despite approval by the Air Staff no order was forthcoming as the new fighter used a version of the Curtiss D-12 in line engine. A proposal was made that the new Rolls-Royce Kestrel F.10 engine be used but weight complications reduced the operational speed.

Upon issue of Specification F.20/27 a second version of the Firefly, the Mk II with the Kestrel engine was submitted for tender to the Air Ministry. It flew for the first time on 5 February 1929 with the designation Mk IIM (metal). Modifications followed, but at 175mph @ S/L it was not as fast as the Hawker Hornet. However, the Belgium Government expressed an interest and it was built by the company in its new factory in Belgium.

> **Leading particulars**
> *Wing span:* 30ft 8in, area 236 sqft. *Length:* 24ft 8in. *Height:* 9ft 1in. *Weights:* tare 2,387lb, gross 3,285lb. *Max speed:* 175mph @ S/L, 223mph @ 3,285lb @ 13,123ft. *Ceiling:* 30,840ft. *Height to time:* 19,685ft in 10min 55secs. *Engine* 480hp Rolls Royce F.XIS (Kestrel).

Gloster SS19B

This was a significant aeroplane as it was the vehicle that was submitted to a number of Air Ministry Specifications that led to F.7/30 and produced the Gladiator. The previous prototype Gloster SS18B was fitted with the Bristol Jupiter VIIF engine to become known as the S.S.19B. Also this prototype was armed with two fuselage mounted Vickers .303in m/gns plus four Lewis guns mounted under the upper and lower wings, an extremely heavy armament for that period. Total ammunition carried was 1,600 rounds, plus provision for four 20lb bombs under the lower wings.

Gross weight rose to 3,520lb and a maximum speed of 188mph attained @ 10,000ft. At Martlesham Heath during trials it was known as the Gloster 'multi-gun fighter'.

It was tendered to F.20/27 and awarded a Contract No. 787177/27 for a single prototype, serial number J9125. It flew for the first time in February 1933 powered by the Bristol Mercury VIS of 520hp. But, it too, was rejected in favour of the Hawker entry.

> **Leading particulars**
> *Wing span:* 32ft 9.5in, area 315sqft. *Length:* 25ft 4in. *Height:* 10ft 2in. *Weights:* tare 2,704lb, gross 3,858lb. *Max speed:* 204mph @ 10,000ft. Landing 59. *Ceiling:* 33,350ft. *Height to time:* 20,000ft in 12.15mins. *Engine/s:* as above.

Saunders-Roe A.10 (Multi-gun) Fighter

The was originally a private venture (PV) entry and the company modified it for tender to the Specification. It was a sesquiplane of all metal construction and made a first flight on 27 January 1929. Despite its lack of performance a Contract No. 74201/30 was allocated, serial K1949, and used for trials to examine the effects of multi-gun firing before being struck off charge in 1933. It had a maximum speed of 200mph, landing 70. The ceiling was 29,000ft, a gross weight of 3,467lb, a single Rolls-Royce F.XI engine of 480hp and was armed with twin .303in Vickers m/gns.

Vickers Type 151 Interceptor, Jockey

This company tendered one of the most modern low wing, constant chord, cantilever monoplanes of the competition and as a result one aircraft was ordered under Contract No. 831868/27. It incorporated the structural design of the all metal Wibault and was powered by a Bristol Mercury IIA radial of 480hp. Vickers called it the Jockey due to its small dimensions and it carried the serial number of J9122.

It was transported by road to Martlesham Heath where it made its maiden flight in April 1930. Vibration of the rear fuselage was cured by modifications and drag reducing spats added. A new Mercury VIS2 replaced the original engine and at one stage a Jupiter VIIF. Local strengthening of the rear fuselage overcame vibration problems. During further spinning trials at Martlesham the prototype crashed.

Westland F.20/27 Interceptor

This was the second wire-braced monoplane tendered to the specification of all metal construction which was accepted by the Air Ministry, who placed a contract for a prototype under Contract No. 813869/27 in January 1928. Design started in late summer of 1927 and J9124 made a first flight in August of the following year. Originally it was powered by a Bristol Jupiter Mk VII radial engine of 420hp, but this was replaced by a Mercury. The original design featured a small area fin/rudder assembly but this was increased in area at a later stage to produce a rather taller unit. It had a wing span of 38ft 0in and length of 25ft 4.5in. With a maximum speed of 192mph it was eliminated from the competition. Gross weight was 3,325lb with two .303in Mk II Vickers guns in the front fuselage.

Westland Wizard Mk II

The Wizard design was just as advanced as the Jockey and the first Westland prototype J9124. This had a wooden fuselage and was powered by a Rolls-Royce Falcon III engine. As a PV the risk was entirely associated with Westland, and when the Mk I version crashed it appeared the design had come to an end. However, the Air Ministry was interested and placed a Contract No. 841676/28 for the Mk II, which had a steel tube fuselage with fabric covered metal wings.

As J9252 it was an interesting design that unfortunately lacked the required performance despite the Rolls-Royce FXIS engine of 500hp. Maximum speed was 188mph @ 10,000ft, a rate of climb of 2,000ft/min @ S/L and a gross weight of 3,275lb. The Rolls-Royce 490hp F engine was also used during trials. Armament of twin Vickers guns and four 20lb bombs.

Insofar as Hawker Aircraft was concerned with F.20/27 Sydney Camm and his team continued the steady development of previous Hawker biplane fighters, introducing no radical or unproven advances from its original design concept, the Hawker Hoopoe.

This aircraft was submitted by Hawker to Naval Specification N.21/26, another Private Venture by Hawker. It was designed around the air-cooled radial Bristol Mercury engine and achieved a maximum speed of 196mph. The Rolls-Royce Company had in the development stages a new in-line engine, the F.XI, and Sydney Camm, Chief Designer of Hawker Aircraft, considered it could be suitable for the Hoopoe. Unfortunately this proved to be too difficult. However, the Hoopoe design and F.XI concept was not abandoned.

The design to F.20/27 followed the line of design of the Hoopoe and was eventually submitted to the Air Ministry in tender form during November 1927. It attracted an award of a contract (No. 813870/27) to develop and construct a single prototype. This

Leading particulars

Design type: Single radial engine, single-bay biplane. Prototype interceptor fighter. *Crew:* One (pilot). *Designer:* Sydney Camm. *Air Ministry Specification:* F.20/27. *Engine:* One 450hp Bristol Jupiter IV, 9-cylinder air-cooled radial engine driving 2-blade Watts 10ft 6in diameter, fixed-pitch wooden propeller (450hp Bristol Mercury also installed). *Fuel capacity:* 50 gallons in internal tanks: *Armament:* Two nose-mounted synchronised Vickers .303in machine guns with 600rpg. *Date of first flight:* 1929. *Pilot:* Flt Lt P.W.S. Bulman. *Delivery:* to Martlesham Heath for evaluation during 1929.

Basic data

Wing span: 30ft 0in, area: 250.7 sqft. *Length:* 23ft 6.5in. *Height:* 9ft 5in. *Weights:* tare 2,340lb (2,363 Mercury), gross 3,150lb (3,178 Mercury). *Maximum speed:* 214mph @ 10,000ft (218mph @ 10,500 Mercury). *Cruising speed:* 180mph (190 Mercury). *Maximum range:* About 470 statute miles at 180mph @ 9,000ft (approx 460 Mercury). *Duration:* 3.10hr. *Climb rate:* 1,980ft/minute (200 Mercury). *Service ceiling:* 27,500ft.(28,000 Mercury). *Prototype registration:* J9123.

F.20/27 Prototype with Bristol Mercury VI, Brooklands 1930. (Hawker Aircraft)

aircraft, J9123, flew for the first time from Brooklands Aerodrome the following August, 1928, with George Bulman at the controls.

The airframe was an all metal structure utilising the recently developed Hawker system. Engine, a single Bristol Jupiter VII, nine-cylinder, air-cooled radial, developed 450hp. Propeller was a standard Watts 2-blade wooden unit. Armament was to be two fixed, forward firing Vickers machine guns.

The prototype was delivered to Martlesham Heath for trials at the end of 1928 with the Watts replaced with a Fairey-Reed, 2-blade metal propeller. Maximum speed with this engine/propeller combination was 190mph, not quite meeting the 200mph @ 20,000ft requirement. J9123 was returned to the Hawker Company in May 1930 for fitment of a new, prototype Bristol engine, the Mercury VI, and further trials took place at Martlesham with the radio compartment deleted as a weight saving device. The aeroplane reached a maximum speed of 202mph thus satisfying the demands of Specification F.20/27. However it was to be subsequently damaged during those trials and the engine sent back to the Bristol Aircraft Company and the airframe into storage.

This brought an end to the first stage of Fury development.

CHAPTER TWO

The Hawker Fury

The decision was taken by the Hawker Company and the Air Ministry that no dedicated Fury prototypes would be manufactured for use as trials aircraft, and that the first three production machines, K1926/27/28, would be regarded as development aircraft and used for service evaluation.

The Fury had arrived at an unfortunate moment in time as the Bristol Bulldog was still in service, and the cost per complete airframe/Kestrel engine was £4,800. As a result only small numbers were eventually delivered.

The first production contract awarded to the Hawker Company (August 1930) was to comply with Specification 13/30 under Contract No. 40559/30 of March 1930 and the name changed from Hornet to Fury. A total of twenty-one examples were constructed and serials of these ran from K1926 to 1946. The engine specified was the Kestrel IIS which developed 525hp @ 14,000ft. Three additional production contracts were also ordered under Contract No. 40559/30 to the same specification and totalled eighty-four machines.

The first flight of production Fury K1926 took place from Brooklands on 25 March 1931. Except for minor differences it was the Hornet with the advanced R-R Kestrel IIS engine, a development of the F.11S and F.12S, supercharged to produce 525hp at 14,000ft and it was to provide the Royal Air Force with its first aeroplane that could reach a speed of 200mph plus. It set new standards of performance; high rate of climb; light on the controls and a fast rate of roll.

The basic structure was a single bay biplane of unequal span, the top wing being 30ft 0in; the bottom 26ft 0in. Centre section was above the fuselage on splayed out struts, and the interplane struts of 'N' formation, had an outward rake from bottom to top wing. Wing spars were manufactured from steel and of polygonal section and single plate webs. Ribs were of spruce and the complete structure covered with fabric. Ailerons were fitted to the top plane only.

A rectangular fuselage was faired into the oval forward section containing the Kestrel engine by means of spruce formers and stringers. This wooden structure was fabric covered. The engine was closely cowled with aluminium panels, and the flush exhaust stubs resulted in the fine lines which were typical of the design.

Elevators were balanced and the tailplane adjustable for incidence. The complete empennage was constructed from metal frames covered with fabric. The wheels were mounted on a cross axle and suspended on oil and rubber compression shock absorbing struts. The whole unit was braced at the rear by means of radius rods. A ventral radiator was enclosed in a fairing which had shutters, these being controlled by the pilot who controlled the flow of air through the matrix.

The standard fighter armament of two, synchronised Vickers .303in calibre machine guns was located in the nose top decking, and each gun had a maximum of 600 rounds. The Fury I was produced in limited quantities and it was an expensive acquisition for the RAF. Only three fighter squadrons, Nos 1, 25 and 43 were initially equipped. Needless to state, they were regarded as the elite.

After K1926 and K1927 had been tested the first Fury batch of twenty-one aircraft had flown in three weeks, followed by the remainder as mentioned above. The Air Ministry returned the J9682 (ex-Hornet) to Hawkers, and it was this aeroplane that was used to demonstrate the type's versatility to overseas buyers in Denmark, Norway, Spain and Yugoslavia. During trials with K1927 a retractable radiator was tested for use with the steam-cooled Goshawk engine. K1926 was modified to Fury Mk I standard and issued to No.1 (F) Squadron based at Tangmere.

The second production batch of Fury Mk Is (Specification 13/30) was for forty-eight aircraft under Contract No. 102468/31. Serial numbers K2035 to K2082.

An interim batch of fifteen Fury Mk Is was ordered under Contract No. 184968/32, in the serial range of K2874 to K2883, K2899 to K2903. This was followed by a fourth batch of thirteen examples under Contract No. 252331/33, serials K3730 to 3742 which went to No. 43 Squadron exclusively at Tangmere and were equipped with Vickers Mk III guns.

A fifth production batch of twenty examples under Contract No. 408396/35, K5662 to K5682 were built in 1935.

Second Prototype Fury Mk I K1927, Brooklands, 1931.

Leading particulars

Aircraft configuration: Single-seat, single bay biplane fighter powered by one 525hp Rolls-Royce Kestrel IB, 12-cylinder engine driving a 2-blade, fixed pitch wooden propeller. *Function:* Prototype interceptor fighter. *Air Ministry Specification:* .303in synchronised Vickers g/gns mounted in the engine cowling to fire forward through the propeller arc. *Date of first flight:* July 1930. *Pilot* P.E.G. Sayer. *Wing span:* 30ft 0in, area 250sqft. *Length:* 26ft 8.75in. *Height:* 9ft.6in. *Weights* tare 2,409lb, gross 3,232lb. *Maximum speed:* 202mph @ 10,800ft. *Cruising speed:* 180mph. *Maximum range:* approx 370 statute miles @ 180mph @ 10,000ft. *Time to height:* 15.25min to 20,000ft. *Service ceiling:* 28,000ft. *Number built:* two Fury prototypes.

Note tare weight of K2927 was 2,623lb, and gross 3,318lb. *Maximum speed:* 214mph @ 13,000ft, cruising 186. *Maximum range:* approx 310 miles @ 180mph @ 12,600ft. *Time to height:* 14.75min to 20,000ft. *Service ceiling:* 28,000ft. No provision for bomb carrying. *Number built:* two Fury prototypes, K1926 and 1927, plus contracts for normal production models.

In the same year that the first Fury Contract was placed (1930) that far reaching Air Ministry Specification F.7/30, that resulted in the Spitfire, was issued. Sydney Camm, too, was working on the Monoplane Fury, that was to evolve into the Hurricane. He was aware that two to three years would pass before even an accepted design was approved by the Air Ministry and he advanced a scheme whereby, as a stop gap, Hawker Aircraft could produce an interim type.

The company agreed upon funds for another Fury Private Venture, which when constructed became (unofficially) known as the Intermediate (or Interim) Fury. The Hawker design team had improved the basic Fury and construction of a prototype was initiated. Registered G-ABSE it flew for the first time on 13 April 1932 with Gerry Sayers at the controls. It was fitted also with a range of 'special' engines; had a cantilever spatted undercarriage with internally sprung wheels. A number of engines were flight tested - Goshawk III (evaporative steam cooling); Kestrel IVS; Kestrel VI and Kestrel Special (VIS), an up-rated Kestrel VI. The Kestrel engine burned a fuel consisting of a special fuel and castor oil to DTD 71.

G-ABSE was built as a standard Fury Mk I but as improvements materialised they were applied to the airframe and engine. These included speed spats; the Kestrel IIS engine was modified to incorporate Rolls-Royce a Goshawk supercharger and a special composite steam and water cooling system was evolved utilising a small steam condenser in the upper wing centre section.

In this configuration, and in preparation for production of the Fury Mk II, G-ABSE was delivered for trials at the Aircraft & Armament Experimental Establishment, Martlesham Heath in May 1933. These tests had to be curtailed due to the unsatisfactory engine running. An indicated air speed of 240mph was recorded before the tests were abandoned and G-ABSE returned to Hawkers at Brooklands.

A second Hawker PV (Fury I) was the 'Intermediate Fury'.

Leading particulars

Aircraft configuration: Single seat, single-bay biplane. *Function:* Company trial installation. *Air Ministry Specification:* Private venture. *Engine:* one 550hp Rolls-Royce Kestrel IIS 12-cylinder composite water and steam-cooled in-line driving a 2-blade Watts wooden propeller. For Martlesham trials a small steam condenser was mounted in the upper wing centre section. The engine was fitted with a Goshawk blower. Fuel was a mixture of a special petrol mixed with castor oil to DTD 71. *First flight:* 13 April 1932. *Pilot:* P.E.G. Sayer. *Wing span:* 30ft 0in, area 250sqft. *Length:* 26ft 8.75in. *Height:* 10ft 2in. *Weights:* tare 2,750lb, gross 3,350lb. *Maximum speed:* 231mph @ 15,000ft. *Cruising speed:* 205mph. *Maximum range:* approx 300 statute miles @ 200mph @ 14,500ft. *Time to height:* 7.41min to 20,000ft. *Service ceiling:* 27.100ft. *Number built:* One prototype, registration G-ABSE.

The Air Ministry expressed an interest in the type and was to issue Specification 14/32 for a 'High Speed Fighter' (modified Fury), or (unofficially) 'Super Fury'. K3586 was modified in 1933 under Contract No. 190683/32 to G-ABSE standards with the spatted undercarriage. It was fitted with Kestrel IIS of 600hp; Kestrel (S) Special Kestrel VI engine, 600hp; Kestrel IIIS, 525hp; Kestrel VIS, 600hp; Goshawk III and Goshawk B.41. It originally appeared with a swept-back upper wing and Vee-interplane struts, as shown in the illustration on page 23, and the Kestrel 'S' engine. The top wing was later to be substituted for one of a more conventional shape and fitted with steam condensers in the leading edge for the R-R Goshawk 3.

With the Goshawk III engine developing 695hp installed, cooling was achieved by seven steam condensers located along the front section of the upper wing. A small, auxiliary, retractable radiator situated below the fuselage was used when the aeroplane was climbing to height. The same system was used on the Hawker P.V.3 and tendered to Specification F.7/30. Performance was inhibited due to the excess weight of the Goshawk cooling system.

It made its maiden flight on 3 May 1933. The official trials were impressive and resulted in the issue of Specification 6/35, as outlined later. At the end of the trials it was converted to Fury Mk II status and issued to No. 43 Squadron as a replacement machine. By mid-1936 it was withdrawn from RAF service and delivered back to Rolls-Royce to become one of the growing numbers of Merlin engine test beds. It ended its days, ignominiously, on a salvage dump near Cambridge.

F.14/32 High Speed Fury (Modified)
Leading particulars
Aircraft configuration: Single engine, single-bay biplane. *Function:* Experimental interceptor fighter. *Specification:* F.14/32. *Engine:* one 600hp Rolls-Royce Kestrel S. *Armament:* two .303in Vickers machine guns mounted in engine cowling and firing forward through propeller arc. *First flight:* 3 May 1933. *Pilot:* Flt Lt P.W.S. Bulman. *Wing span:* 29ft 6.25in, area 250sqft. *Length:* 20ft 6.25in. *Height* 9ft 6in. *Weights:* tare 2,985lb, gross 3,500lb. *Maximum speed:* 245mph @ 1,000ft. *Cruising speed:* 210mph. *Range:* 210 statute miles @ 1,500ft. *Time to height:* 7.4min to 20,000ft. *Service ceiling:* 31,800ft.

It is interesting to note that K3586 was to have a 1,015hp Rolls-Royce Merlin C engine installed by Rolls-Royce. This provided a maximum speed of 265mph @ 17,000ft and was to be called (provisionally) Fury Mk II.

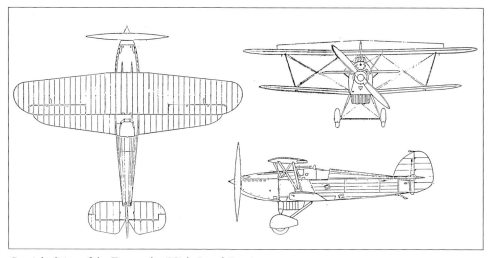

Special edition of the Fury – the 'High Speed Fury'.

Development of the basic Fury continued and Air Ministry Specification 6/35 was for a Single-Seat Interceptor Fighter, the Hawker Fury Mk II, issued in March 1935. One Mk I Fury, K1935 T.I was modified by Hawkers in 1933, to the same standard as G-ABSE with a Kestrel VI engine to flight test the various features of the forthcoming Fury Mk II. In addition to a number of changes it could accommodate additional fuel in internal tanks. Contract No. 421941/35 called for twenty-three aircraft, serial numbers K7263 to 7285. First flight by K7263 was on 3 December 1936.

The same year Specification 19/35 was raised for a second production batch of fifty-seven aircraft sub-contracted to General Aircraft at Hanworth, Middlesex, Contract No. 419059/35, serials K8232 to K8306. The official record read 'Fury Kestrel V (de-rated)'. Both Marks of Fury, I and II, were in service until 1937 until replaced by the Gladiator when the majority were relegated to the RAF Training Schools as advanced flying trainers. Hawker Aircraft was now completely stretched to produce their new monoplane fighter, the Hurricane.

Leading particulars

Dimensions

Wing span: (top) 30ft 0in (bottom) 26ft 0.25in, area 252 sqft. *Chord:* (top) 5ft (bottom) 4ft 10in. *Dihedral:* (top) 1° (bottom) 3° 30in. *Stagger:* 2ft 9.6in. *Tailplane span:* 10ft 0in, chord 4ft 0in. *Length:* 26ft 8.75in. *Height:* 10ft 2in (tail down) 11ft (tail up). *Wheel track:* 5ft 9.5in. *Propeller diameter:* 10ft 6in.

Performance

Maximum speed: 207mph @ 14,000ft, 214mph @ 13,000ft. Landing 65mph. *Height to time:* 20,000ft in 9min 40sec, 10,000ft in 4min 25sec. *Max rate of climb:* 2,350 ft/min. *Service ceiling:* 28,000ft, max 29,200ft. *Range:* 305 miles. *Engine:* One 525hp Rolls-Royce Kestrel 2S, 12-cylinder, 60° Vee, water-cooled. *Fuel capacity:* 50gals (approx). *Weights:* tare 2,528lb, gross 3,350lb. *Service load:* 790lb. *Wing arrangement:* Unequal span, single-bay, staggered biplane. Ailerons on top wing only. *Armament:* Two fixed synchronised Vickers .303 m/gs firing through propeller disc. 600rpg.

Foreign Contracts

Yugoslavia

As early as 1932 the Yugoslav Government had also contracted a licence to build the Fury powered by Hispano-Suiza 12Xdrs engines. This contract was modified when the Yugoslav Government decided to order the H-S powered machine direct from Hawkers, ordering one machine as related. However as the first foreign operator of the Fury, six aircraft were ordered in September 1931 under Contract No. S68281/36/C/4(c), they bore the numbers HF1 to HF6 and were fitted with R-R Kestrel XVI engines.

Leading particulars

Wing span: 30ft 0in, area 250.7 sqft. *Length:* 27ft 5.5in. *Height:* 9ft 6in. *Weights:* tare 3,005lb, gross 3,835lb. *Maximum speed:* 222mph @ 15,000ft. *Cruising speed:* 200mph. *Range:* 350 SM @ 200mph @ 15,000ft. *Ceiling:* 27,400ft. *Armament:* Two 7.7mm Spandau m/gns firing through propeller arc. 1,200 rounds carried. *First flight:* 18 September 1935. *Pilot:* P.W.S. Bulman.

The Yugoslav authorities were also studying a Fury powered by a more powerful Hispano-Suiza engine, but cooling problems resulted in the idea being abandoned and a second batch of Furies was ordered to be powered by the R-R Kestrel XVI engine, with a single strut, cantilever u/c with sprung wheels. Forty were delivered following a first flight on the first production aeroplane on 14 September 1936, and the type was still in service in early 1940.

Among the non-standard requirements specified for the final series of Yugoslav Furies, was the inclusion of mounting points for additional machine guns mounted under each lower wing, firing clear of the propeller arc. Gun firing trials took place with the .303in Vickers and 7.7mm Spandau in two and four gun configurations. The main differences between the standard RAF issue was Kestrel XVI instead of Kestrel VI. Low velocity cowled radiator and elimination of centre section steam condenser. Modified centre fuselage, cantilever u/c and Dowty sprung wheels. Addition of a centre section fuel tank. The tare weight rose to 3,195lb, and gross weight to 4,065lb. Maximum speed was 237.4mph @ 15,800ft. Cruise 195mph. Range 340 statute miles. Ceiling 28,200ft. First flight 17 October 1936 (Bulman). Trials with both Vickers and Spandau guns made no difference to performance. Ten were ordered under Contract No. 568281/36.

Yugoslav Fury, with Rolls Royce Kestrel engine and new, cantilever undercarriage legs.

The final Yugoslav Fury variant was one aircraft (HF.6) being returned to Hawker for the installation of a Lorraine Petrel H frs engine of 745hp. Shipped to Yugoslavia in April 1933.

Leading particulars

Aircraft configuration: Single in-line engine, single-bay biplane. *Function:* Interceptor fighter for Yugoslavia. *Crew:* One (pilot). *Designer:* Sydney Camm. *Specification:* Yugoslav Government Order. *Engine:* One 750hp Hispano-Suiza 12Nb, 12-cylinder liquid-cooled in-line engine, driving standard 2-blade Watts wooden propeller. *Armament:* Twin fixed synchronised 7.7mm Spandau machine guns mounted to fire forward through propeller arc. 1,200 rounds of ammunition. *Date of first flight:* 18 September 1935. *Pilot:* Flt Lt P.W.S. Bulman. *Date of delivery:* Prototype flown to Yugoslavia, 1 October 1935. *Wing span:* 30ft 0in. *Length:* 27ft 5.50in. *Height:* 9ft 6in. *Weights:* tare 3,005lb, gross 3,835lb. *Maximum speed:* 222mph @ 15,100ft. *Cruising Speed:* 200mph. *Maximum range:* About 350 statute miles @ 200mph @ 15,000ft. *Rate of climb:* 2,300ft/min. *Service ceiling:* 27,400ft. No provision made to carry any bomb-load on the Fury. *Number built:* One. *Prototype Registration:* Nil.

Norway

In the opening months of 1932 the Norwegian Government ordered a single Fury for evaluation purposes. Numbered 401, it was powered by an Armstrong-Siddeley Panther IIIA air-cooled radial. It was delivered in September 1932 after making its first flight on the 9th with Bulman as pilot. Negotiations commenced to produce the type under licence. But the radial engine restricted performance and the plan was abandoned. For a short period it was fitted with a ski undercarriage. Subsequent production was at the Army factory at Kjeller.

Norwegian (Panther) Fury, 401 at Brooklands.

Leading particulars

Aircraft configuration: Single-bay biplane with single radial engine. *Function:* Interceptor fighter. *Crew:* One (pilot). *Designer:* Sydney Camm. *Specification:* Norwegian Government Order. *Engine:* One 500hp Armstrong-Siddeley Panther IIIA, 9-cylinder air-cooled radial engine driving fixed-pitch 2-blade propeller. *Armament:* Two synchronised 7.7mm or 13.2mm Spandau machine guns on nose cowling, fixed to fire through the propeller arc. *Date of first flight:* August 1932. *Pilot:* Flt Lt P.W.S. Bulman. *Delivered:* to the Royal Norwegian Air Force About July 1933. *Wing span:* 30ft 0in. *Length:* 25ft 10.50in. *Height:* 9ft 2in. *Weights:* tare 2,825lb, gross 3,500lb. *Maximum speed:* 201.5mph @ 16,400ft. *Cruising speed:* 166mph. *Maximum range:* About 350 SM @ 169mph @ 15,000ft. *Time to height:* 5.25min to 10,000ft. *Service ceiling:* 25,000ft. *Number built:* One in Great Britain. *Prototype Registration:* '401'.

Persia

During 1933, under Contract No. 1001118/33, a small number of Furies (sixteen) were delivered to the Persian Government powered by Pratt & Whitney Hornet S.2 B1G radial engines driving Hamilton 3-blade metal propellers. However, when the first prototype flew on 29 May 1933 it was fitted with a 2-blade, Watts wooden fixed pitch. Immediately after this flight a Hamilton propeller was installed in order comparative trials be carried out. Conclusions reached revealed while the 3-blade version had a better performance in many areas, overheating and supercharger clutch slip was directly attributable to the heavier Hamilton prop. Persia had placed an order in January 1933 for sixteen aircraft, but for some curious reason specified that the Pratt & Whitney 575hp Hornet S.2 B1G, 9-cylinder, air-cooled radial be installed in preference to the S1G unit, plus a Hamilton 3-blade propeller. The combination altered the centre of graity and a number of the Persian Furies nosed over during ground manoeuvres. Serials 201 to 216.

Leading particulars

Aircraft configuration: Single radial engine, single-bay biplane. *Function:* Interceptor fighter for Persia. *Crew:* One (pilot). *Designer:* Sydney Camm. *Specification:* Persian Government Order. *Engine:* One 575hp Pratt & Whitney Hornet S.2 B1G. 9-cylinder single-row radial engine driving 2-blade fixed-pitch Watts propeller. *Armament:* Twin fixed forward-firing synchronised .303-inch Vickers machine guns mounted on nose, together with ring and bead sight. *Date of first flight:* 29 May 1933. *Pilot:* Flt Lt P.W.S. Bulman. *Date of delivery:* First aircraft delivered during November 1933. *Wing span:* 30ft 0in. *Length:* 24ft 8.75in. *Height:* 10ft 2in. *Weights:* tare 2,990lb, gross 3,680lb. *Maximum speed:* 200mph @ 14,500ft. *Cruising speed:* 160mph. *Maximum range:* About 350 statute miles @ 160mph @ 14,000ft. *Rate of climb:* 1,780ft/min. *Service ceiling:* 26,200ft. *Number built:* About twelve (3-bl.props). *Prototype registration:* Nil.

Persian Fury No. 203 with P&W Hornet B2G engine and 3-blade Hamilton propeller.

Six additional Furies for Persia were ordered during May 1934 (Contract No. 366843/34) to be fitted with Bristol Mercury VIS2 engines of 645hp driving 2-blade fixed pitch wooden propeller. The intention was to licence build the variant in Persia with both Bristol and American engines, and a total of forty-two Mercurys were despatched to Persia, but it is not known if any airframes were built.

Leading particulars

Aircraft configuration: Single radial engine single-bay biplane. *Function:* Persian Interceptor Fighter. *Crew:* One (pilot). *Designer:* Sydney Camm. *Specification:* Persian Government Order. *Engine:* One 645hp Bristol Mercury WIS2, 9-cylinder air-cooled radial engine, cowled with exhaust collector ring, driving 2-blade fixed-pitch wooden propeller. *Armament:* Two .303in Vickers synchronised machine guns mounted on top of the nose cowling to fire forward through propeller arc. *Date of first flight:* 1933. *Pilot:* Flt Lt P.W.S. Bulman. *Delivered:* to the Persian Government October 1933. *Wing span:* 30ft 0in. *Length:* 24ft 6.25in. *Height* 10ft 2in. *Weights:* tare 3,060lb, gross 3,633lb. *Maximum speed:* 215mph @ 16,500ft. *Cruising speed:* 184mph. *Maximum range:* About 220 SM @ 190 mph @ 14,800ft. *Time to height:* 10.25min to 15,000ft. *Service ceiling:* 24,000ft. *Number built:* One in United Kingdom.

Portugal

Portugal ordered three Furies, 50 to 52, with Kestrel IIs engines and they were delivered during 1934 after a first flight on 28 May 1934 (by Sayer). Contract No. 331709/34.

Portuguese Fury, No. 51, AT Brooklands in 1934.

Leading particulars

Aircraft configuration: Single in-line engine, single-bay biplane. *Function:* Interceptor fighter for Portugal. *Crew:* One (pilot). *Designer:* Sydney Camm. *Specification:* Portuguese Government Order. *Engine:* One 550hp Rolls-Royce Kestrel IIS, 12-cylinder liquid-cooled in-line engine driving 2-blade fixed-pitch Watts propeller. *Armament:* Twin synchronised .303in Vickers machine guns mounted in the nose, firing forward through propeller. 600 rounds per gun. *Date of first flight:* 28 May 1934. *Pilot:* P.E.G. Sayer. *Date of delivery:* Delivery to Portugal completed during June-July 1934. *Wing span:* 30ft 0in. *Length:* 26ft 8.75in. *Height:* 10ft 2in. *Weights:* tare 2,623lb, gross 3,318lb. *Maximum speed:* 214 mph @ 13,000ft. *Cruising speed:* 191mph. *Maximum range:* About 305 statute miles @ 13,000ft @ 190 mph. *Rate of climb:* @ 2,069 ft/min. *Service ceiling:* 28,000ft. *Bomb load:* No provision made to carry any bombs on the Fury. *Number built:* About twelve. *Prototype registration:* '50'.

Spain

The final overseas customer for the Hawker Fury was Spain. The Government purchased three examples, and plans were laid for production under licence by Hispano-Suiza. The aircraft were built during the winter of 1935-36 and were ready for flight trials the following April 7, 16 and 22. The engine was to be the Hispano 12Xbrs of 700hp. Armament was either the Vickers Mk 5 machine guns or Hispano 7.92 or 13.2mm calibre guns. First flight date of '4-1' was 7 April 1936, with the last flying on the 23rd of the same month. The three aeroplanes arrived in Spain on 28 April 1936 just days before the civil war erupted. They were numbered 4-1, 4-2 and 4-3. Spanish Furies fought all through the civil war and two survived.

Spanish Fury with Fascist forces during the civil war, 1937.

Leading particulars

Aircraft configuration: Single in-line engine single-bay biplane. *Function:* Interceptor fighter for Spain. *Crew:* One (pilot). *Designer:* Sydney Camm. *Specification:* Spanish Government Order. *Engine:* One 700hp Hispano Suiza 12Xbrs, 12-cylinder liquid-cooled in-line engine driving 2-blade fixed-pitch propeller. *Armament:* Two 13.2mm synchronised Hispano-Suiza guns mounted on top of the nose cowling to fire forward through propeller arc. *Date of first flight:* 7 April 1936. *Pilot* Flt Lt P.W.S. Bulman. *Date of delivery:* to Spain, first three aircraft 28 April 1936. *Wing span:* 30ft 0in. *Length:* 26ft 8.75in. *Height:* 9ft 6in. *Weights:* tare 3,005lb, gross 3,800lb. *Maximum speed:* 234mph @ 13,400ft. *Cruising speed:* 180mph. *Maximum range:* About 300 miles @ 180 mph @ 13,000ft. *Time to height:* 7.50min to 20,000ft. *Service ceiling:* 28,000ft. *Number built:* Three evaluation aircraft Registration: 4-1, 4-2, 4-3.

South Africa

The stories of Furies to South Africa are many and sprinkled with rumour. Records made available to the author reveal that South Africa received eighteen Furies, together with spares, during 1938. This consignment was made up of Furies from the second production batch having a mixture of tail skids or wheels. It was the intention to despatch additional Furies direct from storage at RAF Sealand during 1939. They were never shipped to South Africa and all stored Furies were scrapped during 1940. The Fury Mk II in SAAF service served with more squadrons than did the Mk I and II during their seven years of service with the RAF.

Specification 29/34 was seven aircraft (200 to 207) under Contract No. 354486/34 of 21 September 1934. The first six, serial numbers K3733, 3735, 5663, 5669, 5670 and 5672, were delivered on 1 January 1940. A single aircraft, K5674, was delivered on 5 August the same year. The following month, on the 5th, 2050, 2071, 2877, 3731, 3739, 3740 and 5676 were delivered. On the 6 September K1929, 3741, 5675 and 5678 arrived, and the final four machines, K2899, 2903, 2875 and 5680 were delivered on 7 October 1940.

The first SAAF squadron, No. 1, was equipped with Furies and Hurricanes and they moved into East Africa to counteract the Italian threat to Kenya. When the Italians became involved in the Second World War the Squadron was divided into three flights with the Fury acting as escorts to the Hawker Hartbees.

No. 2 Squadron was Fury equipped and both squadrons operated from landing grounds against the Italian Forces. No. 4 Squadron used the Fury as a trainer and No. 13 was the third Fury outfit. The final unit to operate the Hawker fighter was No. 40 equipped with Fury and Hartbees. The last operational use of SAAF Furies was in 1942.

The South African Furies were fitted with the Kestrel VI and had a tare weight of 2,736lb. Service load and fixed equipment totalled 316lb. Fuel 50 gals, oil 4.25 gals @ 421lb. Fully loaded 3,601lb.

According to records RAF serials K4863 to 4869 under the same contract were annotated 'for SAAF, re-allotted', but a number of RAF Furies were transferred to SAAF during 1940 and numbered as 208 to 228.

Leading particulars
Fury 2
Specification: 14/32 (production 6/35). *Prototype:* K1935. *Squadrons:* 1, 23 and 43. *Wing span:* 30ft 0in, area 252 sqft. *Length:* 26ft 8.75in. *Height:* 10ft 2in. *Maximum speed:* 196mph @ 5,000ft; 223mph @ 15,000ft; 220mph @ 20,000ft; 215mph @ 23,000ft; 191mph @ 30,000ft. *Landing:* 62.5. *Time to height:* 3.8mins to 10,000ft. *Service ceiling:* 32,000ft. *Absolute:* 32,800ft. *Range:* 460 miles. *Weights:* tare 2,734lb, gross 3,700lb. *Engine:* One 700hp Rolls-Royce Kestrel 6, 12-cylinder 60° Vee steam-cooled supercharged. Crankcase cooling, 7-element oil cooler. Auto boost control. *Cooling system:* Steam condenser in nose section of top wing, plus water header system. *Wing arrangement:* as Fury I. *Production:* first K7263, last K8292.

The Hawker PV3 Fury

The Hawker Fury design represented the pinnacle of biplane interceptors that were operated by the Royal Air Force. It was fast, well armed and the favourite mount of the young pilots of the 1930s. For them it was their Spitfire, and only the elite squadrons were equipped with them.

When invited to submit entries to Specification F.7/30, Sydney Camm decided to propose a private venture type that was, in effect, a Fury with the Rolls-Royce Goshawk engine. Initially, he had installed the engine in a Fury, K3586, then a civil Fury, G-ABSE – the Intermediate Fury – and that same airframe was to become the High Speed Fury, or Super Fury, in preparation for the PV3 to observe performance of the aeroplane with the parallel chord upper wing fitted with steam condensers.

K3586 'High Speed Fury'.

The High Speed Fury (K3686) flew for the first time with the new engine and a four gun armament of two Vickers mounted in the nose section above the exhaust manifolds and two under. Camm had visited Rolls-Royce for discussions in the August of 1931 when the decision was taken to fit a more powerful Goshawk into the completed PV3 airframe. Two were delivered to the Kingston Works as B41 and B43 during May 1935, and the first (B41) was flown in the PV3 airframe on 26 June. A second aircraft took to the air on 9 July.

In 1936 the aeroplane, now designated as I-PV3 and powered by the B43 engine, was

Hawker I-PV3 with Goshawk III evaporative cooled engine.

delivered to Martlesham Heath for trials. Unfortunately the Gloster Gladiator had now been ordered as the winner of Specification F.7/30, and there was no official requirement for a second biplane fighter. However, experience with the two aeroplanes was to prove of immense value to Camm in the Hurricane development.

PV3
Leading particulars
Wing span: 34ft 0in, area 290sqft. *Length:* 28ft 2in. *Height:* 10ft 5in. *Weights:* tare 3,530lb, gross 4,670lb, max permissable 4,850lb. *Max speed:* 224mph @ 14,000ft. *Ceiling:* 29,600ft. *Height to time:* 10,000ft in 4mins 20secs; 20,000ft in 12mins 5secs. *Engine:* Rolls-Royce Goshawk III, steam-cooled of 695hp; later B41 and B43 engines of 700hp. *Propeller:* 2-blade wooden Watts fixed pitch or 3-blade metal Fairey Reed of fixed pitch. *Fuel* 70gals. *Armament:* four forward-firing .303in machine guns with 1,800 rounds of ammunition.

Furies Mk I of No. 43 Squadron, serial batch 1926 to 1946. Squadron colours were black checks on silver dope.

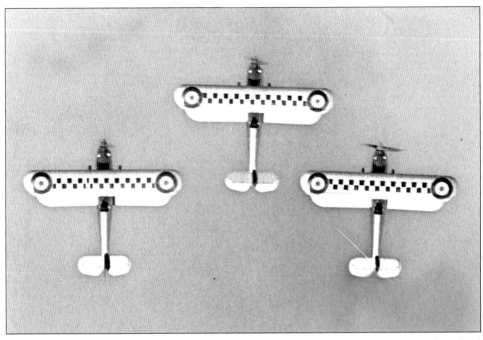

Overhead view of No. 43 Squadron Furies. Tailplane of Flight Leader's aircraft has yellow fixed section.

Side view of No. 1 (F) Squadron's Furies. K2048 is the CO's aircraft.

Fury Mk Is of No. 1 (F) Squadron, in neat formation.

CHAPTER THREE

Birth Pangs

Fury to Hurricane

The 1930s ushered in the Great Depression when the American economy was halted as the banks demanded money for shares purchased on a margin. It came to an end with the outbreak of the Second World War. It was also the period that witnessed the demise of the biplane fighter, constructed of a wooden airframe covered with canvas, and led to the metal skinned monocoque structure.

A number of successful aeroplanes were designed and produced including the famous twins of the Battle of Britain, the Hurricane and Spitfire. When Supermarine tendered for the Air Ministry contract, F.7/30, their Southampton factory was working well under capacity. A contract to build a prototype fighter, with the possibility of a substantial production run, would have been most welcome.

The meeting that initiated the design of the Hurricane took place in the boardroom of H G Hawker Engineering Company in March 1929, almost ten years before it was so urgently required. Among the personalities gathered around the table were the company directors, design staff members and engineers and an Air Marshal, Sir John Salmond. Of the assembled men he was the key figure as his choice of the aircraft manufacturer to design and develop the next generation of RAF fighters would be crucial, both to England and the Hawker Company.

Salmond was to be shown a prototype of the company's latest fighter, the Hornet, with its estimated maximum speed of 200mph. The Air Marshal was not impressed as the fighter was yet another step along the road of biplane design. What he considered to be the next generation was an all-metal, multi-gun, monoplane fighter.

Hawker's great rival, Supermarine, were also working on fast monoplanes but Hawker's Chief Designer, Sydney Camm felt the need for caution and careful progress towards that goal. In 1930 Salmond was appointed Chief of the Air Staff and one of his senior officers was Hugh Dowding, later to be appointed to the post of Air Member for research and development to produce the policy of acquiring new aircraft equipment for the RAF.

Fighter design was at a crossroads the world over and the chilling forecast of Stanley Baldwin, Britain's Prime Minister, that 'The bomber would always get through', concentrated the political minds to such a degree that that the public purse strings were loosened. England recognised the truth of this bleak prophecy in a positive manner, with the Air Ministry issuing a Specification for a day and night fighter capable of speeds of 250mph and armed with four machine guns. The demand was a spur to the aircraft industry to finance research and development, and it must have come as a great disappointment when the F.7/30 contract was awarded to Gloster Aircraft for yet another biplane fighter, the Gladiator.

Mitchell's F.7/30 design was the Supermarine type 224 monoplane, a rather clumsy open cockpit fighter with gull wing and trousered undercarriage. It used the troublesome evaporative cooled Goshawk engine with its complicated cooling system and was a total failure.

Camm's entry, again cautious and still a development of the Fury, was the Hawker PV3, an enlarged Fury with the Goshawk Mk II of 695hp and cooling radiators occupying most of the upper wing leading edge. Aerodynamically it was excellent. Weight-wise it was a failure as was its cooling system was complex and susceptible to battle damage. It had a maximum speed of 220mph.

There was a plus factor, for the Specification was to produce the initial impetus which would lead to the emergence of the Hurricane and Spitfire. Mitchell's first attempt at an all-metal, cantilever wing, day and night fighter was to experience a complete metamorphosis to the type 300.

In 1933 Camm and his design team were investigating schemes for a single-seat fighter to replace the Fury and at that period the design of the biplane was capable of further development with a new engine. However, any development of the Fury would be limited to a maximum speed of approximately 250mph. Anything with a higher performance than this figure had to be a monoplane with a cantilever wing.

Camm regarded airframe development as a step-by-step process and, having eliminated a redesigned Fury, turned his attention to the monoplane. This design eventually evolved as a clean, fixed undercarriage configuration utilising the fuselage and tailplane of the existing Fury but with a single wing. His choice for the engine to power this new design fell, once again, to the Goshawk but, as many designers at that time discovered, this was to prove a disaster. This new aircraft had an internally braced wing of some 200sqft and spanned 38ft. The pilot was also provided with a covered cockpit.

The only jarring feature was the long, spatted undercarriage with internally sprung Palmer wheels and a spring-loaded moving axle to absorb landing shocks. The new design was called the Fury Monoplane and it had an estimated maximum speed of 280mph. An alternative engine, the Bristol Mercury VI radial, was proposed but rejected. The Goshawk powered aircraft had a gross weight of 3,807lb and, with the Mercury, 3,709lb.

Sydney Camm received details of the PV12, recognised that it was a better engine than the Goshawk and without its faults, and started design of the High Speed Interceptor Monoplane which eventually evolved into the Hurricane to Specification F.36/34.

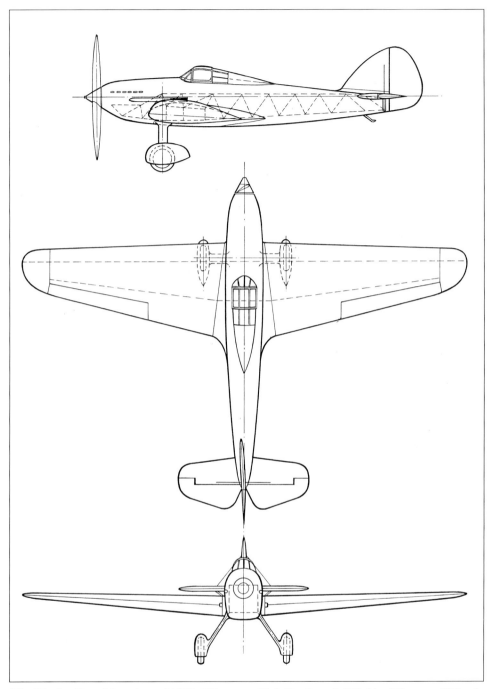

The Hawker Fury Monoplane of 1933. Wing span 38 ft 0in. Length 28ft 0in. Wing area 200 sqft. Loading 19lb/sqft.

F.36/34 Prototype

If Mitchell's Spitfire was the product of inspired genius, then Sydney Camm's Hurricane was the outcome of rational development. Both fighters were ready in quantity at the time when England faced her greatest peril – during the summer of 1940.

Sydney Camm's next attempt was to the Specification F.5/34. First thoughts: a 'Fury biplane engineered to accept the new Rolls-Royce Merlin engine monoplane' (of 1933), virtually a cantilever monoplane derivative of the Fury, with the new Rolls-Royce Kestrel engine and fixed undercarriage. A maximum speed of 270mph was estimated. A variant was the same Fury type with a retractable undercarriage. However, when drawings of the new design were shown to Dowding in October 1933, Camm could not persuade him that a Goshawk-powered, monoplane Fury variant was a better proposition than the Gladiator.

The third design, was for a four-gun monoplane. An enclosed cockpit and retractable undercarriage were considered essential to meet the demands of Specification, F.5/34, which was to transform the shape of British fighters. Both the Spitfire and the Camm Fighter included the design requirements, and in June 1933 a one-tenth scale model of Camm's thoughts of a monoplane fighter was tested in a wind tunnel. A complete Specification was referred to the Air Ministry the following August as an 'Interceptor Monoplane'.

Initially the Rolls-Royce Goshawk was still favoured as a promising engine, but it was soon overtaken by the Rolls-Royce PV12 (later to be named the Merlin). Four machine guns, originally specified for the F.7/30, were the chosen armament mounted in the fuselage, but this was increased to eight with the adoption of some features of Specification F.5/34. All these requirements were satisfied in an airframe that differed little in structural design from that of the Fury. The fuselage was still fabricated with metal formers and stringers, and fabric covered. The cantilever wings, built as a Warren truss between Hawker dumbbell spars, were also fabric covered. There was one great fault, the undercarriage was fixed and had spats covering the wheels. Construction posed no great

Prototype Hawker F.37/34 (Hurricane) K5083, in its original form with wheel cover flaps, braced tailplane and single pillar canopy.

problems even for a newly recruited work force.

A conference was held at the Kingston Works with Air Ministry personnel on 10 January 1934, during which a full-scale mock-up was examined. This originally featured an armament of four Vickers machine guns, but successful negotiations to produce the American Colt Browning led to the provision for an eight gun battery in the wings outboard of the propeller arc. The prototype contract, No. 357484/34, was received by the Hawker Aircraft Company on 18 February. Three days later detailed performance figures arrived at the Air Ministry.

Referred to in company records for almost two years as the 'High Speed Interceptor Monoplane', the prototype of Camm's new fighter got under way early in 1935 and estimates of performance included an maximum speed of '330mph with the aid of a Rolls-Royce Merlin of 1,025hp at 15,000 feet'.

By August 1935 the prototype, K5083, was structurally complete at the Kingston factory and the new Merlin C (No. 11) installed. Guns were not installed but ballast carried in lieu. Skinning and system tests occupied six weeks, and on 23 October the aeroplane was moved to the Hawker assembly plant at Brooklands for engine running and taxiing checks. Weighing of the fully loaded prototype disclosed that the centre of gravity lay within half an inch of the designed location. On 6 November the silver monoplane was ready for flight and on that day Flight Lieutenant P.W.S. (George) Bulman lifted it from the grass of the famous airfield at a gross weight of 5,420lb.

Difficulties with the Prototype

Not long after the K5083 started its flight trials it received a setback. News was received that the Merlin C had failed to pass its rigorous fifty-hour civil test and trouble was experienced with engine No. 11 in the prototype. The aircraft was grounded during January 1936 while engine No. 15 was installed and other modifications carried out. These included minor alterations to the cockpit hood and the radiator bath. Performance measurements were undertaken on 7 February and a maximum speed of 315mph was achieved at 16,200 feet. The gross weight now increased to 5,670lb with a radio installed.

K5083 was flown to A&AEE, Martlesham Heath, on 18 February to gain initial Service impressions, but trouble was still experienced with the engine, supercharger bearings and valve springs being the most frequent cause of failure. The prototype was the first interceptor to exceed 300mph. It had, however, already been decided to discontinue development of the Merlin C, and later versions were planned for production aircraft. Meanwhile engine Nos 15 and 17 had failed, and K5083 returned to Brooklands with No. 19.

The Hawker Board of Directors were confident that with favourable comment from the evaluation pilots, led by Squadron Leader D.F. Anderson, the new fighter would eventually be ordered into production. It was decided, in March, to set in motion the necessary steps to build the aeroplane in quantity. They therefore, and quite arbitrarily, ordered jigs and materials for 1,000 aeroplanes. However, on 3 June their confidence was justified by receipt of Contract No. 5217112/36 for 600 aircraft, the largest single peacetime order yet placed, and on 27th of the same month the name 'Hurricane' was selected.

The airframe was a single-seat, low wing, cantilever monoplane with a retractable undercarriage and enclosed cockpit. It was powered by one Rolls-Royce Merlin engine driving a Rotol or de Havilland constant speed propeller. The wing was built in three sections – centre, port and starboard with split, trailing edge flaps situated between the inner ends of the ailerons. Covering was initially fabric, to be later replaced by metal. Main fuel tanks were in leading edges of wings with a third in the fuselage ahead of the cockpit.

F.36/34 prototype
Leading particulars

Wing span: 40ft 0in, area 258sqft. *Length:* 31ft 6in. *Height:* (prop vertical) 13ft 6in. *Weights:* tare 4,129lb, gross 5,672lb. *Wing loading:* 22lb/sqft, power 5.5lb/hp. *Max speed:* 316mph @ 15,000ft; 270mph @ S/L. *Ceiling:* 33,600ft. *Height to time:* 5,000ft in 2min 2sec; 30,000ft in 22min 30sec. *Landing:* 57mph. *Range:* 525 miles. *Engine:* Rolls-Royce Merlin C of 1,025hp @ 3,000rpm @ 11,000ft; 905hp @ 2,400rpm @ 9,800ft. *Propeller:* Watts, wood, 2-blade Z33 of 11ft 6in dia. *Fuel:* 107.5gals. *Armament:* Eight .303in Browning m/gns.

Three-quarter rear of K5083 shows the broad chord Watts, wooden propeller and wing walkways.

Prototype in flight reveals the small ventral radiator bath and braced tailplane.

K5083 pictured at Brooklands shortly after roll-out, late October 1935. Note wing walkways and other markings.

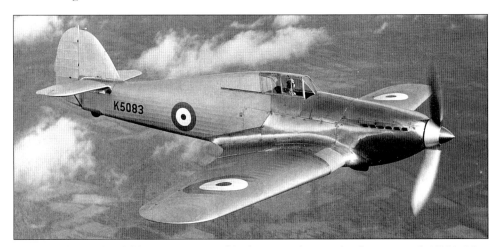

Front metal covered and fabric rear covering of fuselage in evidence in this flying view of K5083. Note cockpit canopy has been strengthened with additional frames.

K5083 after Martlesham trials in 1937. Armament installed, radio mast, ring and bead sight.

CHAPTER FOUR

The Mark I Series

The production facilities at Kingston and Brooklands were insufficient to cope with the rush of orders and the company raised a loan to purchase Parlaunt Park Farm, at Langley, to build a new, enlarged factory. The first production Hurricane emerged from this plant in 1938.

Meanwhile the prototype underwent intensive flight trials and modification. The wheel D-flaps were removed as were the tailplane struts; the canopy further strengthened by the addition of side struts. Service radio was installed and Merlin C, No. 15, re-rated at 15,500 feet, was installed and this bestowed a speed of 318mph. The landing flap centre section, which extended behind the radiator venturi, was removed as it was suspected this impaired engine cooling when lowered for landing.

In December 1936 it had been decided to discontinue the Merlin I in the Hurricane

Heart of the Hurricane was the centre section to which the u/c legs were attached and outer wing panels. Forwards of the fire wall was the engine mount.

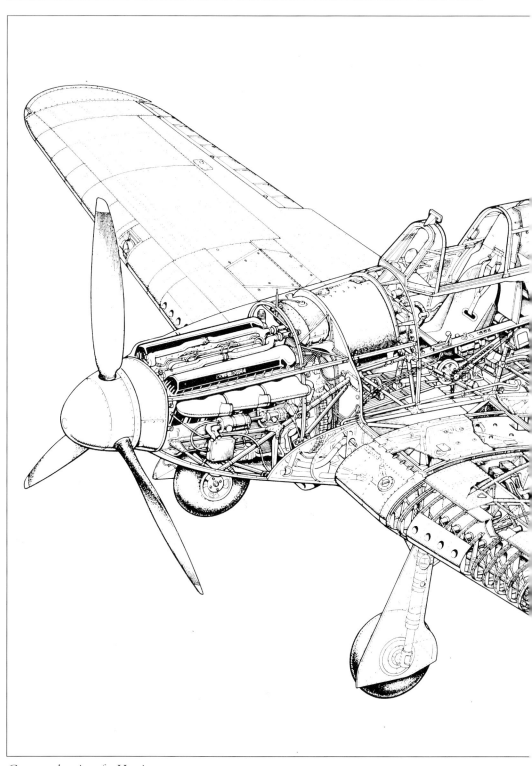

Cutaway drawing of a Hurricane.

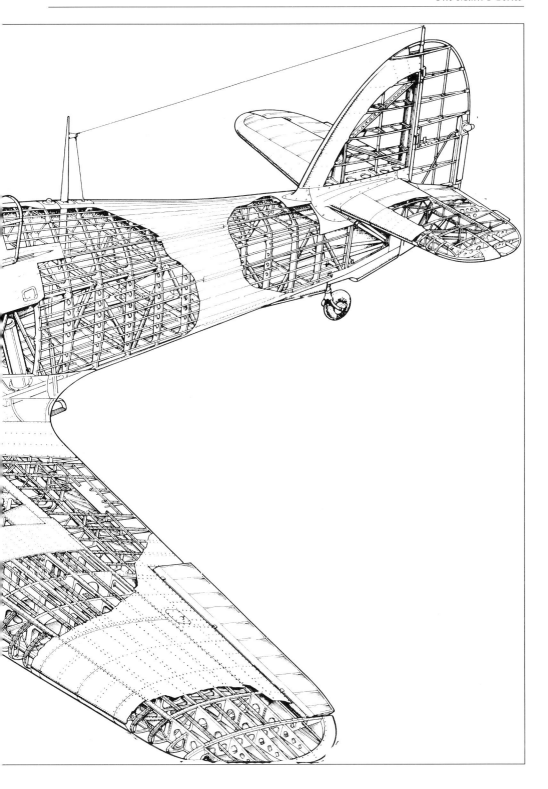

and Spitfire production and to concentrate on the Merlin II (developed from the Merlin G), and this change, although fully justified by later events, necessitated almost six months' delay in the assembly line. With the introduction of the inclined rocker box flanges; reshaping of the glycol coolant tank and improvement of the engine starting system, the entire nose profile of the Hurricane had to be redesigned.

To assist in tooling up for production, Merlin G, No. 7, was delivered to Kingston and installed in the first production airframe, L1547, on 19 April 1937. The Production Specification P.15/16 had been placed with Hawker on 20 July 1936. The prototype in the meantime had undergone preliminary spinning trials; armament and gunsight had been fitted and numerous production features incorporated.

The first flight by L1547 was made on 12 October with Philip Lucas at the controls and, by the end of November, six more aircraft had flown. In the late 1930s there were no Maintenance Units where RAF aeroplanes could be delivered for fitting equipment, and it was fairly common practice to deliver new aircraft to RAF squadrons straight from the factory. The first squadron selected to receive the new Hurricane was No. 111, based at Northolt, and by Christmas they had received four aircraft.

By the end of February the squadron had taken delivery of its initial quota of sixteen Hurricanes (L1548-L1561, L1563 and L1564), each of which had to make six flights before delivery. On 10 February, possibly spurred by news that Germany had recently established a new World Speed Record, No. 111 Squadron's Commanding Officer, Squadron Leader John Gillan, decided to demonstrate his new fighter's performance to the world. He flew to Turnhouse, Edinburgh, against a headwind that reduced his average

The first squadron to have the Mk Is was No. 111 when based at Northolt. Note all props centre horizontal. Kidney exhaust ports.

speed to 280mph. On the return journey, aided by a strong tailwind (which was scarcely mentioned at the time), he flew from Turnhouse to Northolt at an average ground speed of 408.75mph.

The second Hurricane Squadron was No. 3 at Kenley (S/Ldr H.L.P. Lester) whose aircraft (L1565-1573, L1576-L1580, L1582, L1586-L1588) arrived in March 1938. No. 56 Squadron at North Weald (S/Ldr C.L. Lea-Cox) was next with L1584, L1590-L1595, L1597-1603, L1605-L1611.

Thus, by mid-1938 RAF Fighter Command had received about fifty of the eighty Hurricanes completed so far. But improvements to the Mark I were being constantly developed by the manufacturers. Towards the end of 1937 Service spinning trials had disclosed some difficulty in spin recovery resulting from rudder deficiency, and this was extended three inches lower; a ventral spine added under the rear fuselage and the tailwheel fixed in the down position. These alterations were made to production aircraft from about March 1938 onwards.

The 2-blade, fixed pitch, Watts wooden propeller was replaced by a two position, Hamilton, 3-blade metal propeller, first flown on L1562 in July 1938. The same aeroplane was used to introduce an armoured bulkhead ahead of the pilot. Further armour protection, including a bullet-proof windscreen, flown in L1750, was incorporated later.

Development of the Rotol 3-bladed, constant speed propeller, prompted Hawkers to acquire an RAF Hurricane (ex-L1606, now registered G-AFKX), in which was installed a Merlin III engine, No. 11111. This engine came to be adopted by all future Hurricane Is and Spitfire Is as it possessed a universal propeller shaft capable of accommodating either the DH variable pitch or Rotol constant speed propellers. Now powered by the Merlin III, and armed with eight .303in Browning machine guns, the Hurricane had a top speed of 328mph at 16,200 feet, and could climb to 15,000 feet in 6.2 minutes.

Hurricane Mk I, L1762, No. 313, was shipped to Canada as trainer in October 1938.

Munich and After

Up to the crisis of Munich in September 1938 production of the Hurricane progressed at a slightly faster rate than could be accommodated by Fighter Command's re-equipment plans, and Hawkers were authorised to pursue foreign sales of the aircraft to nations considered likely to resist the current Nazi territorial adventures. Early production Hurricanes attended air shows on the Continent and, not surprisingly, attracted attention from other nations. Yugoslavia ordered a dozen and deliveries started on 15 December 1938. Belgium ordered twenty, the first of which left Brooklands in April 1939. Romania placed an order for twelve.

But the writing on the wall at Munich lent urgency to Fighter Command's re-arming. Henceforth, the call was to increase production to create a substantial reserve from which newly formed squadrons could draw, not to mention the need to meet demands made by the first Auxiliary Air Force Squadrons. They, it was planned, should convert to Hurricanes and Spitfires, and so become fully integrated within the air defence system.

As the 1930s drew to its close, war in Europe once again appeared inevitable as Germany threatened the peace of the world with its demands for living space. In England preparations were under way in 1937, albeit at a slow rate. As part of the armaments build up the Royal Air Force had revealed to industry Expansion Scheme E, which outlined an enormous aircraft programme in order to be able to re-equip its old and new squadrons with the necessary aeroplanes. A total of 800 aircraft had to be completed by the end of 1937, of which 500 were to be fighters, including the Hurricane.

By May/June 1938 the production rate had risen to five aircraft per week. In September 1938 the programme for re-equipping Hurricane squadrons had reached a total of twelve by the time of the Munich Crisis of that month when it was disclosed that only two squadrons were fully operational. Nevertheless the RAF brought all its squadrons up to readiness. Production was accelerated but fortunately the crisis passed over when Czechoslovakia was partitioned.

However, the writing was on the wall and production of both the Spitfire – which was lagging badly – and the Hurricane were stepped up. Nos 73, 32, 1, 43, 79 and 151 were equipped to be followed by Nos 213, 501 and 504; the latter being Auxiliary Squadrons which normally would be equipped with second line fighters. But the auxiliary pilots had honed their skills when flying at weekends and during holidays. They were all soon absorbed into Fighter Command.

At the outbreak of war 18 Hurricane squadrons were fully operational by day, and 3 others were in the conversion process. Of the original Hurricane order of 600 aircraft, 497 had been completed, but already new contracts for 900 Hurricanes had been placed, of which 600 were to be built by the Gloster Aircraft Company, a division of Hawker Siddeley. Most Hurricanes were being completed with fabric-covered wings in the interests of maximum production, but new, metal-clad wings were beginning to emerge from Brooklands and these were retrospectively fitted as aircraft returned for major maintenance or repair. The first Hurricane with metal wings was L1887. Other experimental Hurricanes that flew before the war included L1750, fitted with two, 20mm cannons under the wings, L1669 tropicalised with carburettor sand filter and L1696 with slotted wings.

Hurricane Mk IIA, Series 2. P3269. Merlin XX engine. Langley Airfield Defence F/F July 1940. Motto 'Death Clutching Swastika'.

VY-H of No. 86 Squadron, RAF Debden, 1939. Squadron insignia is on the fin.

The Battle of France

With German storm troops supported by armour and clouds of *Luftwaffe* fighter and medium bomber squadrons the full picture of *Blitzkrieg* was revealed to the world. It seemed the lessons of the Spanish Civil War had been ignored by the world, in which German fighter and bomber pilots had learned the art of war when competing against second rate aircraft such as those supplied Russia.

It appears to historians that the Royal Air Force appeared to ignore the method of interception and fighter sorties by the German *Luftwaffe*, which soon adopted new methods of support for each other without resorting to the clumsy 'Vic' formations, a 'V' of fighters with 'tail-end Charlie' keeping a lookout for enemy intercepting fighters attacking from the rear. Charlie was normally the first to go before the remainder of the squadron felt the full fury of the attack. It was not until the hard lesson was learned during the Battle of Britain that the 'finger-four' method was adopted.

Among the RAF's immediate reactions to the declaration of war was the despatch of four Hurricane squadrons to France, Nos 1 and 73 accompanying the Advanced Air Striking Force, and Nos 85 and 87 providing the fighter element of the Air Component of the British Expeditionary Force. Two squadrons of the Auxiliary Air Force, equipped with Gladiators, Nos 607 and 615, were converting to Hurricanes when the German attack in the West was launched on 10 May 1940. Air activity over the Western Front had been sparse during the first eight months of the war, the so-called 'Phoney War', the first German aeroplane to fall to RAF guns in France was a Dornier Do17, shot down by Pilot Officer P.W.O. 'Boy' Mould, of No. 1 (Fighter) Squadron, in Hurricane L1842 near Toul on 30 October 1939.

No. 1 Squadron was based at Vassincourt, No. 79 at Rouvres and Nos 85 and 87 at Lille/Seclin. There were also PRU Spitfires that roamed the battlefields for up to date information on the position of German forces.

War in a entirely separate area of the world resulted in a number of Hurricanes being

Mk Is of No. 85 Squadron, Air Component, France, December 1939. VY-G.

Hurricane base (Mk Is), France, 1939/40.

hurriedly prepared for delivery to Finland, and so scarce were the fighters that Hurricanes were drawn from front line service with Nos 19 and 20 Squadrons and shipped to Finland in February 1940. However, they never fought with the Finnish Air Force as Russia and Finland had agreed an armistice.

In the opening months of 1940 German forces invaded Norway to protect its shipments of iron ore and in April that year captured the port of Narvic. Churchill also planned to capture the same port and despatched eighteen Hurricanes aboard HMS *Glorious* together with the supporting ground crew and pilots from No. 46 Squadron. They landed at Skaanland on 27 May where they soon went into battle with the *Luftwaffe*. After three aircraft had been damaged in Skaanland, the remaing aircraft were moved to Bardufoss, near Narvik, covering British ground forces in the area.

Several German aircraft were shot down during the next week but the situation was hopeless as enemy pressure increased by land, sea and air. On 3 June the British evacuation began and on 7 and 8 June the ten surviving Hurricanes were flown onto the *Glorious.* Volunteers pilots were being asked to accompany their aircraft home, only to be lost within twelve hours when the carrier was sunk by the *Scharnhorst* and *Gneisenau*. Of the twelve pilots, only S/Ldr K.B.B. Cross and Flt Lt P.G. Jameson were rescued from the Arctic waters and brought safely home.

Returning to France it was on 10 May 1940 that the German Army and *Luftwaffe* broke the resistance of the Low Countries and invaded France. There were a number of Hurricane squadrons active in France including Nos 1, 73, 85, 87, 607, 615 with a strength

France, 1939/40. Mk Is of No. 73 Squadron, No. 67 Wing, Advanced Air Striking Force. Majority of Mk Is were written off during that period.

of ninety-six aircraft.

The crushing defeat by German forces which burst upon France and the Low Countries on 10 May, brought about the swift destruction of the Dutch and Belgian Air Forces. The onrush of the *Wehrmacht* through Belgium exposed Northern France, and the British Expeditionary Force (BEF) was forced back to the Channel Ports. In answer to frantic appeals by France, three more Hurricane Squadrons were despatched across the Channel, Nos 3, 79 and 501, but with scarce vestige of control and organisation, little could be done to stem the *Luftwaffe* attacks. The RAF Squadrons fell back across France, fighting where and when they could, and destroying perhaps a hundred enemy aircraft. However, in the three weeks of fighting, the nine Hurricane Squadrons lost, or were obliged to destroy, twice that number of their own aircraft. The main hazards lay in the inappropriate duties given to the Hurricane pilots, such as that of escorting almost suicidal raids in conditions of enemy air superiority, while servicing facilities on the ground were almost non-existent.

Losses among the British squadrons were average for the number of sorties flown during which they destroyed a good number of *Luftwaffe* aircraft, and Dowding released a further thirty-two Hurricanes after the entire Belgium force of Hurricanes had been caught off the ground and destroyed by enemy attacks.

As the fighting progressed so the British squadrons were forever retreating from base to base, burning those Hurricanes which could not be saved. Dowding's reinforcements were soon being destroyed and he was under constant pressure from Churchill and the War Cabinet to ship further aircraft. He resisted, fiercely stating that he had already sent to France more than a third of his Home Defence Squadrons and that it was futile to allow the enormous drain of his Hurricane squadrons on a hopeless cause. Churchill listened and agreed and Dowding conserved his precious Hurricane and Spitfire force with which to defend England. Dowding

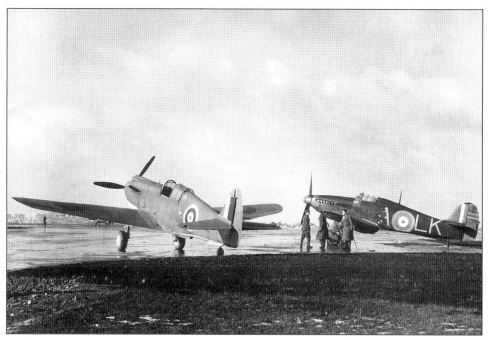

Mk I, LK-A, No. 87 Squadron in background with P-40, France.

knew that France was defeated and that England would be next. He wanted to be ready to take part, with Fighter Command, in beating off any planned German invasion.

The last batch of Hurricanes based in France with Squadrons Nos 1, 73 and 501 left the Continent in the final days of May after burning any aircraft that could not fly back to England. The most serious consequences of the Battle of France insofar as Dowding was concerned was the loss of 398 Hurricanes and 200 pilots either killed, missing or severely wounded. Replacing these men was much harder than replacing aeroplanes.

Early Mk I, France 1939 to '40. Returned to UK to become night fighter. Matt black overall.

Home-based Hurricanes flying from Biggin Hill did take part in the air battles over France and acted as escorts to Blenheim bombers' offensive patrols in an endeavour to halt the German forces. No. 32 Squadron was in the thick of the fighting and, considering the overwhelming number of *Luftwaffe* aircraft, managed to maintain a high average by shooting down more of the enemy than they lost themselves.

Dowding rotated his squadrons, relieving Nos 32 and 79 at Biggin Hill and switching No. 610 to the Kent airfield together with Nos 213 and 242 for covering the retreat from Dunkirk. It was Air Marshal Keith Park's No. 11 Group that once more provided cover for the trapped British and French forces but, due to their restricted range, the Spitfires and Hurricanes could only patrol the area for forty minutes before having to return to Southern England. As Park only had sixteen squadrons to work with there were times when no air cover was available, leading to the BEF complaint that the RAF ignored their plight. On one day alone Hurricanes shot down ten Bf109s for the loss of two, and often the overworked squadrons were sent to France as many as five times each day, returning only to refuel and rearm. For five long days Operation *Dynamo* was actively saving the beleaguered troops and by the evening of 4 June it was all over. In nine days of fighting Hurricanes from Biggin Hill alone had destroyed thirty-six German aircraft for the loss of fourteen. In addition many more many German bombers and fighters had been badly damaged. Hurricanes also flew from Lympne, Manston and Hawkinge from where they also provided air cover during the smaller evacuations from Brest, Cherbourg, Nantes, St Malo and St Nazaire.

L1592 in the period when it was with No. 56 Squadron at North Weald and No. 45 at Tangemere during the Battle of Britain. Note the large grey codes, four colour fuselage rings and fin stripes.

A captured Hurricane I, V7670, in German markings. This aircraft was abandoned by the Germans in North Africa during March 1941.

During the Norwegian campaign it was planned to fit RAF fighters with floats as they lacked long-range capabilities. These Blackburn Roc floats designed to fit a Hurricane were, in fact, never used.

The first Hurricane to be fitted with a tropical filter seen here at Martlesham in 1939. This was 'Collie's Battleship', L1669, shipped out to the Sudan at the end of 1939 and named after Air Commodore Raymond Collishaw.

Hurricane fitted with Smoke Curtain installations foe laying smokescreens during combined operations.

Many schemes were tried in an attempt to conserve fuel on longer hauls. This Hurricane is fitted with a 'bridle' and line to enable a towing aircraft, once airborne, to pull the aircraft with its engine turned off.

CHAPTER FIVE

The Battle of Britain

The events that constituted the Battle of Britain are too well known to warrant detailed description here except insofar as the outcome of the great battle was to a greater extent dictated by the Hurricane, despite its inferior performance to that of the Bf109 and Spitfire.

When the battle opened at the beginning of July, Fighter Command deployed twenty-eight and a half Hurricane squadrons, compared with seventeen and a half squadrons of Spitfires. All but one of the Hurricane squadrons were operational, albeit tired and resting after Dunkirk, whereas two Spitfire squadrons were regarded as trials units, and four others were only operational by day. Seventy-two percent of all Hurricane pilots had seen combat, compared with only twenty-six percent of the Spitfire pilots. Moreover, the Spitfire was still in advance of universal maintenance standards in Fighter Command, with the result that during July and August only eight airfields in No. 10, 11 and 12 Groups were fully equipped and competent to repair a Category 1 damaged Spitfire. This imposed appreciable limitations on the deployment of Spitfires, as well as inevitably influencing pilots of slightly damaged aircraft in their choice of landing grounds.

Little wonder, therefore, that Dowding chose to weight his fighter defences, in the vital No. 11 Group, in favour of the Hurricane. It was by now a 'do-anything, go-anywhere' fighter, whose structure was of such familiar design that scarcely an airframe fitter in the RAF could have failed to patch up a damaged aircraft. Thus the decision taken by Hawkers, to push on with production in 1936, was amply vindicated.

As the Battle of Britain progressed it was apparent that though the German objective – the annihilation of Fighter Command – was clearly defined, the means were ineptly pursued. The *Luftwaffe* possessed a weapon, the Messerschmitt Bf109E, that properly wielded might alone have destroyed the defending fighter strength, at least in the crucial South East Sector. Certainly, except in very experienced hands, the Hurricane was no match for the 'Emil'. But Göring chose to squander his bomber forces, using them to lure the British fighters into the air, and those bombers operated exactly within the altitude band in which the Hurricane flew best.

July was relatively a quiet month and according to the German *Luftwaffe* was not part of the battle, being restricted to English Channel Convoy attacks in an attempt to bring Fighter Command to battle. But Park, C-in-C of No. 11 Group, was experienced enough to resist pitching RAF fighters against the *Luftwaffe*'s Bf109s.

Among the heaviest days of fighting was 9 July when Convoy patrols were ordered to

Ground crew and Mk I PP3886. No. 56 Squadron, North Weald, June 1940.

protect six convoys and at 12.45 radar stations on the coast reported a build up of German aircraft over the Pas de Calais. Six squadrons were brought to Available and at one o'clock six Hurricanes were ordered into the air. They were climbing to altitude when they sighted over one hundred *Luftwaffe* aircraft overhead.

The Hurricanes attacked, disregarding the odds, to meet the mass of Bf109s and such was the fury of their attack that the Germans broke before the onslaught and scattered. No ships were hit. A second heavy German raid was launched and nine Hurricanes of No. 79 Squadron, plus a number of Spitfires chased after the attackers. A final assault consisted of a number of Ju87 Stukas accompanied by Bf109s which attacked Portland.

Two days later it was overcast and there was little activity during the morning apart from reconnaissance aircraft. At mid-morning a group of Ju87s escorted by Bf110s flew towards Portland to make a successful attack before Park could react. But a number of British fighters met the home-going enemy aircraft and pressed home their attack. A third attack against Portsmouth with Heinkel 111s was intercepted.

There was a quiet period lasting from the 11 to 20 July, during which several daily raids took place with small numbers of attackers. On the 20th a British convoy was proceeding through the Channel under the umbrella of No. 238 Hurricane Squadron. As it went on its way Park became aware of increased enemy activity and ordered two Hurricane and two Spitfire squadrons into the air. At six in the evening a gaggle of Ju87s appeared with a large fighter escort and the ensuing melée started with the Hurricanes diving out of the sun from altitude taking the German fighter pilots by surprise. The dog fights spread across the sky and eventually there were eleven British fighter squadrons engaged. Their losses were light with eight British fighters shot down and fourteen German aircraft.

German activity continued throughout the month and ended with a small raid on the 31st. On 1 August Dowding had 60 squadrons available of which 30 flew Hurricanes. In the vital Southern area protected by Nos 10 and 11 Groups he had 28 and a total of 340 Hurricanes, a better position than that of July 1st. However, August was to see an increased weight of Luftwaffe attacks and the official launch date of Eagle Day (*Adler Tag*) – 13 August.

Thursday 2 August was busy but not out of the ordinary with only three British fighters damaged or destroyed. This state of affairs changed abruptly on the following Thursday (8th). A large convoy of approximately twenty ships were being escorted through the Channel by the Royal Navy and the C-in-C *Luftflotte 3* ordered a mass attack. 57 Ju87s protected by an equal number of German fighters had reached the Isle of Wight when 18 Hurricanes dived out of the sun on the packed formations.

However, the Bf109s and 110s fought back fiercely as the dive bombers struck the convoy sinking 4 ships and damaging as many again. The ensuing dog fight of 150 enemy and British pilots spread over a large area, and when the raiders departed for home they left behind 9 aircraft plus numerous others damaged. The RAF lost 2 Hurricanes.

The British convoy re-assembled and proceeded on its way but was attacked for a second time under a cloud of British fighters. By mid-afternoon the Germans returned with 82 Ju87s and almost as many fighters. The British fighters had been waiting, so struck first and soon broke up the enemy attack, but not before the ship convoy had suffered badly with the loss of 7. Although the German aircraft had been badly mauled they were on the credit side. 11 Hurricanes shot down and 20 German aircraft, plus 22 damaged.

The Germans rested their aircraft, apart from sporadic raids, for two days before returning on Sunday the 11th. It was a warm sunny day and the plots were soon appearing on the radar scopes resulting in a raid of 50 plus Ju88s and 20 Heinkels escorted by 30 German fighters. Number 11 and 12 Groups ordered off their aircraft making for Portland and within minutes the fighters from both sides were exchanging shots leaving the deadly bombers to do their work.

They struck vital targets but were to be engaged by the later arrival of British reinforcing fighters. As the fighting spread the German fighters did their best to protect their bombers but like their British counterparts they were low on fuel and ammunition. 36 German aircraft for the loss of 33 British. It was not a good day for Fighter Command.

Enemy pressure was kept up the following day with 27 German and 21 British aircraft destroyed and more was to follow as Eagle Day dawned on 13 August. The German raids began early in the morning when Eastchurch was bombed. Hours later, in the afternoon, 150 German aircraft consisting of Ju88, Bf110s and 27 Ju87s, with a close escort of 109s crossed the Isle of Wight to reach Southampton to be met by 77 British fighters but the city was heavily bombed.

In a separate raid Ju87s were flying towards the Middle Wallop airfield when they were met by fighters which took a heavy toll of the dive bombers. Another target was the airfield at Rochester which was undamaged. It was a day when the *Luftwaffe* had roamed the countryside at will but had paid for their adventures with the loss of 35 aircraft compared to the RAF's 14.

The following Wednesday was quiet, though not with incident, but on the next day it appeared that the whole German Air Force was out. The first raid was against Portsmouth which was met by Fighter Command and there followed a planned attack against British airfields. Ju87s gathered over France with their Bf109 escorts and they were met over Hawkinge when the Hurricanes attacked the Ju87s at low altitude leaving the fighters to the Spitfires.

Lympne was successfully attacked as was Manston and after lunch the Germans prepared their Squadrons for an attack on Dishford and Usworth airfields, with diversions to Newcastle and Sunderland. Unfortunately for the Luftwaffe their intelligence sources had informed them that any opposition would be light and as a result the long range Bf110s were delegated as escorts.

As the raid approached across the North Sea so the British fighters were waiting. 100 enemy aircraft were sighted and attacked from behind with Hurricanes of No. 79 Squadron falling upon the raiders. Twenty per cent of the raiding force was destroyed. The second raid was made by a number of Bf110s against the research airfield of Martlesham Heath which was bombed heavily. Deal was the next target by Bf109s and also Eastchurch. Rochester was bombed and bombs fell upon the Short Bros aeroplane factory.

Sussex and Hampshire had their share of raids with targets such as Hawkinge, Maidstone, Dover, Rye, with the attackers on Worthy Down getting a mauling. Portland attracted a raid by Ju87s which were met by Hurricanes. Croydon was badly damaged with a large number of casualties among the personnel.

In a day when 2,000 enemy sorties had been launched with some degree of success and at cost of 61 aircraft lost, the RAF squadrons lost 30 Hurricanes and Spitfires.

If the 15 August had been critical and hard on the defences, the next day – Friday the 16th – was as bad. By mid-morning the enemy battalions built up over France and a total of approximately 300 fighters and bombers made for the South Coast. Park launched 30 Spitfires and 21 Hurricanes to prevent the raiders attacking once again the vital airfields. Unfortunately for one squadron, No. 266 they lost a lot of pilots and aircraft when caught by surprise by a greater force of Bf109s.

Tangmere was attacked to be met by Hurricane squadrons Nos 1, 43 and 601 and the Spitfires also took on the German fighters. However, Tangemere was flattened even though the Hurricanes shot down 7 Ju87s and damaged 3. The radar station at Ventnor, Isle of Wight, was put out of action for over seven vital days. As dusk approached another large mass of German bombers and their escorts appeared on the radar screens and Hurricanes of Nos 1 and 615 together with No. 64 Squadron's Spitfires intercepted the Germans as they made their way towards Biggin Hill. Most of the *Luftwaffe*'s efforts against Fighter Command's airfields did little damage other than to make a numbers of holes in the grass despite their destroying the airfield's buildings.

A total of 46 German aircraft were destroyed and on the British side 27. Saturday was very quiet due to the weather, but Sunday appeared to offend the *Luftwaffe* as they launched a number of heavy attacks preceded by reconnaissance flights. Shortly after

Sunday lunch had been cleared from British tables the Dover radar reported a built up of enemy forces and at one o'clock Biggin Hill was again attacked to be met by Hurricanes of Nos 32 and 610 Squadron. Out of a total of 9 Dorniers 2 were immediately shot down, 2 badly damaged to crash in the Channel and 3 force landed in France.

A follow up attack by Ju88s on Biggin caused little or no damage as the grass airfield absorbed the bomb blasts. Kenley was also under attack by a very large force and, although intercepted, managed to severely damage the airfield. An hour or so later another raid was spotted as it approached the Isle of Wight, where the German squadrons generally split up. They attacked the radar stations at Poling and the naval airfield of Gosport. At the Poling station 12 Hurricanes of No. 12 Squadron went for the Ju87s as they dived on the target and a total of 16 were shot down after Hurricanes and Spitfires from four squadrons clawed the escorting fighters from the sky. As the daylight faded the Germans launched one of the favourite dusk attacks upon Manston destroying 2 Spitfires.

Five more German squadrons converged upon Kent to make for Croydon but the Germans, upon meeting defending British fighters, turned away. Losses for the day were 43 for the RAF and 60 German, a ratio that disturbed Dowding as the German forces were larger than his and he could not afford to trade blow for blow.

The following three days were quiet with few incidents but as the weekend approached so the Germans became more active and the day promised to be good flying weather. At breakfast time the German raiders began to gather their forces and attacked on a wide front. Twelve defending squadrons could not make much penetration as only two managed to break through the escorting fighters.

After lunch they came again, bombing Manston once again and Hornchurch. At one time No. 11 Group, the most vital in the defence of the Home Counties were out of touch as all communications were cut. The telephone engineers, working under fire, managed to restore them in two hours. North Weald was next when a large formation of He111s, Ju88s and Dorniers were met by British squadrons. No. 151 Squadron's Hurricanes attacked the He111s despite being harried by the German escorts and North Weald escaped with minor damage. No. 10 Group had been called upon to help defend No. 11's airfields but failed to get their aircraft airborne in time. The bombers got through to Portsmouth and caused considerable damage once again.

Losses on both sides were high but the Luftwaffe appeared to be gaining the upper hand. This, however, was to change dramatically with 25 British fighters in exchange for 32 German aircraft. The attrition rate was against the British. The next day, Sunday, was busy but not to that extent with 16 British and 21 German aircraft destroyed. The Monday produced almost equal losses but it was this day that was to witness a divergence of German efforts and ultimate defeat.

Reconnaissance aircraft had revealed to the German C-in-C that large numbers of British fighters were concentrated in No. 11 Group and he sent over the first of many raids. A large group of fighters and bombers crossed north of Dover with some attacking Folkestone. 40 Hurricanes and 30 Spitfires engaged the enemy and the battles raged along the coast from Canterbury to Maidstone. At one time only 7 Spitfires were fighting 50 Bf109s. 5 more, followed by 7 were shot down.

The second raid of the day followed with the German force being intercepted over Colchester as they made for Debden which was bombed without much damage. The third attack saw a group of He111s heading for Portsmouth and eight squadrons of Spitfires and Hurricanes rose to intercept. 22 Hurricanes and 10 Spitfires caught the raiders and turned them away. 24 British were exchanged for 37 Germans.

On the final day of August the *Luftwaffe* continued its pattern of attacking Southern England on a weekend and on this Saturday the radar reported a breakfast raid at eight o'clock heading for Kent. Four waves of German bombers and fighters headed in towards the coast as thirteen fighter squadrons were scrambled. As the Hurricanes met the German formation near Colchester they were engaged by the Bf109 escort and 4 of their number were lost without any gain.

North Weald and Duxford were the apparent targets and a number of Hurricanes were vectored towards them attacking a group of Dorniers. Debden was attacked again but was not stopped from operating at full strength. Eastchurch was bombed for the third time. Biggin Hill was attacked also by He111s and a number of buildings were destroyed without any menace to the grass airfield. As they left the scene the Heinkels ran into a group of Hurricanes. At 5.30 Ju88s and Bf110s attacked Hornchurch and Biggin. Casualties for the day were 34 British and 39 German. As Dowding observed, 'Our young men have to shoot down twice as many of the German young men to keep on an even footing.' Fighter Command was losing the battle, unbeknown, fortunately, to the Germans.

The tired British Squadrons had 31 Hurricanes available on 1 September – not enough. Although this month was the most critical for England as Hitler had ordained that it was to be invaded, fortunes took a turn due to a small raid upon the German capital of Berlin by British bombers. Smarting under the blow Hitler informed Göring to throw his bombers against London. England was saved by that decision, so narrow was that margin.

A snapshot of British squadrons on 1 September revealed Dowding's dilemma, as damage to Fighter Command airfields was severe and the number of first class pilots a diminishing force. Of aircraft he had plenty as the factories and repair shops made good his losses.

He regrouped his squadrons, withdrawing the mauled units from the South and exchanging them for the undamaged ones in the North, whose pilots were also refreshed and had some additional training.

At approximately ten o'clock on the first Sunday in September the Kent radar stations picked up the beginnings of a heavy raid that, upon approach, to the coast split into two major sections which attacked Biggin Hill, Detling, Eastchurch and – for the first time – London. At around eleven o'clock, 12 Hurricanes took off from Croydon for Hawkinge and met, and fought off, a number of Bf109s.

Throughout the day a number of small attacks took place until 5.30 p.m. when the last, expected, raid reached Biggin Hill again. It was a highly damaging attack and almost put the station out of action. It took a great deal of effort by civilian engineers to get it back into service once again. The day ended with the loss of 17 British and only 8 Germans. It was not one of the best days for Fighter Command.

On Monday the 2nd the first German raids took place around eight in the morning attacking Biggin, Rochford, Eastchurch and North Weald. Slowly but surely the German *Luftwaffe* was systematically destroying the airfields of Southern England. At noon a second, larger concentration of German aircraft headed for England and were intercepted by 70 Hurricanes and Spitfires. Despite this number the Germans saturated the British defence and it was followed up by the normal 5.30 raid when 70 Hurricanes and 15 Spitfires met the largest formation of enemy aircraft to date.

Unfortunately it turned into a dog fight and one group of Hurricanes ran into a trap as they climbed to attack a group of Bf109s. It was obvious the *Luftwaffe* was using different tactics by luring the British fighters to engage overwhelming numbers of 109s. Brookland and the Vickers works were attacked for the first time. Dowding and his associate commanders knew the Germans had launched their biggest attacks, throwing everything into the fight to beat Fighter Command before the planned *Sealion* invasion. On that Sunday the RAF lost 25 fighters, compared to the German's 29 and the Germans had still retained huge forces.

On Tuesday 3 September the *Luftwaffe* ranged further abroad striking at Cardiff, Castle Bromwich, where the main Spitfire factory was positioned, Liverpool and Manchester – all at night. Dowding also changed tactics as he transferred the majority of his pilots from the North to Southern England. He had to have sufficient experienced pilots to meet the new German threat. It could have been both adversaries' last throw of the dice.

The biggest German attack of the day started at breakfast time and due to delay in marshalling their forces the Germans ran into stiff opposition by Spitfires and Hurricanes. However, the force consisted mainly of fighters and the RAF avoided and combatted the obvious trap. More enemy aircraft were flying north to first attack North Weald almost destroying it. Large numbers of Hurricanes from Nos 1, 17, 46, 249, 257 and 310 Squadrons engaged the German bombers as they turned for home but they lost heavily. 16 German aircraft lost in exchange for 18 British.

Wednesday brought no respite for the weary pilots of Fighter Command as the seemingly inexhaustible supply of squadrons of the *Luftwaffe* continued to be thrown at them. They attacked Liverpool with little or no opposition at night and turned their attention to the aircraft factories. Without a fresh supply of new fighters Dowding would finally lose the battle. During the day Canterbury, Faversham, Reigate, Redhill and Eastchurch were all attacked. However, Hurricanes of No. 253 Squadron met them under more favourable conditions and shot a number down, but not before a part of the German formation dropped six large bombs on the Vickers works that produced the Wellington. However this aircraft factory was part of the dispersal scheme and little damage was done to the supply of the bomber.

The Kent raiders had been heavily engaged successfully and the survivors limped home. 21 British casualties and 22 German. The odds were stacking up against Dowding. Thursday and Friday, the 5th and 6th of September saw heavy raids by the Germans. The German C-in-C sent over twenty-two separate formations keeping Park and Brand on

Squadron Leader Stanford Tuck leads No. 257 Squadron Mk Is. Based Coltishall, winter 1940.

their toes, meeting such attacks by a force of a 100 aircraft near Hornchurch. 8 Hurricanes ploughed into the attack.

On the following day the oil tanks at Thamestown were blasted and fired by Ju87s. 9 Hurricanes were attacked by diving Bf109s and lost 5 of their number. Over the two days of battle the RAF lost 44 fighters and the Luftwaffe 59.

Saturday 7 September was the vital day for Fighter Command as Göring had been instructed by Hitler to launch an all out attack on London. After the normal reconnaissance flights the German formations did not appear until later in the day and it was not until 18.00 hours that the first plots appeared on the operations boards of Dowding's stations.

The German formations were the largest ever to be launched with hundreds approaching in a stately mass towards the largest target in Europe – London. Park quickly ordered eleven squadrons into the air and within minutes a total of twenty-one were awaiting the invaders. When the British pilots first sighted the awesome mass of enemy aircraft they realised a daunting sight, a virtual tidal wave of bombers and fighters. The Germans must have been reassured and confident they were at last winning the greatest air battle of all time.

All the uncommitted British squadrons guarding the airfields were thrown into the attack, as there was only one target, and with their comrades they smashed into the mighty German mass as the bombs rained down on the East End of London. Many will remember that time vividly, the civilians standing in the streets, witnessing the destruction of their city.

High above London the fighters clashed and it was the Germans that gave way first, beginning the long flight back to bases in France together with their charges, looking anxiously at the rapidly emptying fuel tank gauges. A look at the casualty list for the day tells the story of 31 RAF losses to 37 *Luftwaffe* – still more was to come. The following day both sides rested and the days passed with sufficient air activity to realise the battle was not yet over and decided. The 11 September was a hard day for both Fighter Command and the *Luftwaffe* as the latter again headed for London. There is little doubt the German pilots were facing their toughest test. If the month of July was the Overture to the Battle, August the Fugue, then the Crescendo had to be the month of September. On the 11th neither side gave quarter. In the afternoon the enemy forces headed for another testing time and as a group of He111s approached the beleaguered city they were fallen upon by a mass of 60 Hurricanes and Spitfires which tore the formation apart. The day's losses were RAF 31, Luftwaffe 26. Friday was fairly quiet as the weather was unsuitable for a mass daylight raid, as was the Saturday.

The Hurricanes did great execution among the He111s, Do17s and Ju88s during the first six weeks until the Bf109s were released for 'free chase' sweeps over Southern England, and that was the moment when the fighter defences of England started to suffer most grievously. True, the bomber squadrons still flew with escorting fighters but, between 26 August and 6 September, large and small groups of Bf109s were given free rein to sweep the British skies. They timed their arrival to catch the Hurricanes and Spitfires on the ground or returning from combat when they would be low on fuel and ammunition. In those twelve days the Hurricane squadrons alone lost 134 aeroplanes, or the equivalent of seven squadrons. 35 pilots were killed and 60 wounded. The Command's losses were being suffered at the rate of one squadron every day.

After *Reichsmarschall* Göring's fatal shift of emphasis on 7 September and the resumption of heavy bomber escorts, Fighter Command was able to conserve their fighter strength, and the tide of battle turned back. While never an advocate of the big fighter wing in defence, Air Marshal Keith Park (commanding No. 11 Group) did start to pair his squadrons, when conditions allowed, towards the end of the battle, with the result that, while Spitfires engaged the escorting Bf109s, the Hurricanes fought the bombers. By the end of October 1940 Fighter Command deployed no fewer than thirty-two Hurricane Squadrons, including two Polish (Nos 302 and 303) and two Czech (Nos 310 and 312).

The day of history, Sunday 15 September, had dawned fair without any hint of what was to come. Coastal patrols had been mounted in anticipation of the breakfast attack but all was quiet until almost eleven o'clock. All squadrons in the three Groups brought their squadrons to readiness and any patrolling fighter was ordered to land and refuel. The scene was set for the most critical day of the battle.

Mk Is, No. 306 'Torunski' (Polish) Squadron, Battle of Britain. Note Polish insignia in codes.

The main force of German aircraft was intercepted before it had crossed the coast, thirty-five minutes later and as it attempted to press forward to London so the squadrons rose to join battle. With London in sight the German crews could have expected a slight tailing off of the interceptors in order to avoid the gun barrage, but this day was different. There was no barrage and as the huge bulk of the German attack almost reached London a force of nine squadrons of fighters struck simultaneously, with four Hurricanes meeting the bomber and fighters head-on as another five hit from the side.

The German fighters could not aid their comrades in the bombers as they were busy attempting to defend themselves. Without a moment's loss of speed the whole German bomber force wheeled over London dropping their bombs at random and fled for the coast and France. They were chased across the Channel and the victorious Fighter Command fighters landed for a quick refreshment, refuelling and re-arming, standing ready for the next, expected, big raid.

It came between one and two o'clock as the *Luftwaffe* chiefs thought they would catch Fighter Command off balance. As the bombers and their escorts made their way across Kent they were once again subjected to attack from a fleet of British fighters which went for the bombers as the German fighters attempted to defend their charges.

Thinking that Fighter Command had exhausted its fighter strength the German force ploughed on towards London once again, where they were met by no less than 5 Hurricane squadrons and 6 Spitfire – 300 in total strength. The bomber pilots hurriedly released their bombs over the south-east outskirts of London and turned away to dive towards the coast once again. They were totally demoralised as they had been led to believe that on this day Fighter Command would finally crack. The truth was quite the contrary and Dowding's force was at last at full strength and he still had the Northern Reserves.

A sudden attack by fighter bombers was anticipated as it made for the Spitfire factory at Woolston and the factory escaped without damage. The numbers of aircraft lost by both sides were RAF 26, *Luftwaffe* 60. At those odds Fighter Command could claim the victory.

The battle did not end on 15 September, but from that point on it was no longer conducted at a pace that favoured the *Luftwaffe*, and through the quieter days Fighter Command's strength grew. A big raid took place on 27 September which was launched at 8.15 a.m. It was composed almost entirely of bombers as they had missed their escorts and as they crossed the Channel the German force of 50 bombers was at the mercy of 120 fighters. 24 RAF fighters were lost as compared with 50 German and those totals were to continue throughout the rest of the month. On the penultimate day of September the Germans launched another heavy daylight raid against the whole of the Southern coast and London but there were too many RAF fighters and all the raids were met before they had the chance to reach their targets. The RAF lost eighteen and the Germans forty-two, a ratio that no air force would continue to accept.

The raids continued throughout the whole month of October but they were generally at half, or less, strength of those of September. Hitler abandoned any idea he might have held of invading England and turned his forces towards Russia. The expressed intent was to defeat the Russian giant in six weeks and then build up strength to again subdue the British nation. He had badly miscalculated and within four years stood on the brink of

Mk I, XR-J, No. 71 Eagle Squadron, Kirton-in-Lindsey, Lincolnshire.

Sgt Clisby with his aircraft, P3395 Mk I, No. 1(F)S, Wittering, October 1940. Shot down a Bf109 over Tonbridge, Kent.

total defeat by the Allies. He declared war on America and thus sealed his fate.

There will never be another scenario like that of the Battle of Britain. A single atomic missile or aircraft getting through the defences will destroy any city, even that as large as London. The 'Few' had won a unique victory that proved without any doubt that a well planned and executed defence can hold, and turn back, an attack that consists of greater numbers.

The Hurricane and Spitfire performed in the manner for which they were designed and operated. The total number of Hurricanes destroyed was 507 with probably the same number damaged, the majority of which would have been repaired and returned to Fighter Command. For all that its performance was acknowledged as inferior, the Hurricane gained staunch affection among its pilots. It proved capable of absorbing heavy battle damage and was relatively simple to repair. Its wide undercarriage track allowed landings on hastily repaired grass runways and, being almost viceless and simple to fly, was selected to equip the great majority of the new squadrons. It was, moreover, a match for the German *Zerstörer*, the Messerschmitt Bf110 escort fighter, and proved the point by destroying almost twice as many as the Spitfire. Many damaged Hurricanes were returned to service by the Civilian Repair Organisation (CRO), with a grand total of 661 repaired.

At the end of October the German bomber raids reduced quite drastically and Air Chief Marshal Sholto Douglas realised that, with the pressure removed from the Hurricane and Spitfire squadrons, the RAF could now take on an offensive operation and, in the early months of 1941, produced a plan to carry the air war to the *Luftwaffe* units based in France.

Squadron Leader R.R.S Tuck in his Hurricane Mk I. July 1941. 'Burma' flag and Peacock insignia.

There were many operations which could be broken down into different methods of attack. 'Rhubarbs' designated low level sorties by a small number of fighters to find and destroy targets of opportunity such as trains – in particular locomotives – bridges, anti-aircraft sites, road convoys and barges. A 'Circus' was the provision of a large number of fighters escorting bombers which was aimed at bringing the *Luftwaffe* fighters up to battle. 'Ramrods' were to provide cover and protect bombers for tactical raids. 'Roadstead' was an attack against enemy shipping and 'Rodeos' a sweep by a large number of fighters. The Hurricane was also used for night fighting, without much success.

The following tables list the Hurricanes lost in the Battle of Britain on a daily basis and known enemy aircraft destroyed by the Hurricane. (Date of action, Squadron No. Serial No. (if known) of Hurricane lost and total (T) of enemy destroyed in the day.)

---

4 July: No. 79, No. 601, L1936 (T2). **5 July:** No. 238, P3703, No. 242 (T2). **6 July:** P9444 (T1). **7 July:** No. 79 (T1). **8 July:** No. 32, (T1). **9 July:** No. 43, No. 151 (T2). **10 July:** No. 111 (T1). **11 July:** No. 111, No. 145, No. 501, P3681 (T3), **12 July:** No. 79 (T2), No. 85, No. 151, No. 257 P3767, No. 263, No. 501 (T7). **13 July:** No. 56 (T2), No. 238 P2950, No. 263 (T4). **14 July:** No. 615 (T1). **15 July:** No. 17, No. 213, No. 249 (T3). **19 July:** No. 1 P3471, No. 32, No. 43 P3140, P3531 (T4). **20 July:** No. 32, No. 43 P3964, No. 238 P3766, No. 263, No. 501 (T5). **21 July:** No. 43 N3973 (T1). **22 July:** No. 85, No. 601 P1772 (T2). **23 July:** No. 3, No. 232 P3641, No. 257 P3641 (T3). **24 July:** No. 46, No. 151 (T2). **25 July:** No. 43 N2665 (T1). **26 July:** No. 87 P3596, No. 501 P3808, No. 601 P2753 (3). **27 July:** No. 87 (T2). **28 July:** No. 245, No. 257 P3622 (T2). **29 July:** No. 43 L1955, No. 56 (2). **31 July:** No. 501 (T2).

1 Aug: No. 145 P3155 (T1). **6 Aug:** No. 232 R4090 (T1). **7 Aug:** No. 501 (T2). **8 Aug:** No. 43 (3), No. 145 (5), No. 238, No. 238 (2), (T11). **9 Aug:** No. 605 L2103 (T1). **11 Aug:** No. 1, No. 17, No. 56 N2667, No. 87 (2), No. 111 (5), No. 145 (3), No. 213 (2), No. 238 (4), No. 601 (4), P38783, L2057, R4092, P3885, No. 615 N2337 (T24). **12 Aug:** No. 32, No. 56, No. 145 (3), No. 151 (2), No. 213 (2), No. 257 (2) P3776, P3662, No. 501 (12). **13 Aug:** No. 43 P3972, No. 43, No. 56 (4), No. 87, No. 151, No. 213, No. 238 (3) (T12). **14 Aug:** No. 43 L1739, No. 615 (2) (T2). **15 Aug:** No. 1 (3), No. 17, No. 32, No. 87 (2), No. 111, No. 151 (3), No. 257 L1703, No. 501 (2), No. 601 (2) P3232 (T18). **16 Aug:** No. 1, No. 43 (2) L1736, N2521, No. 111 (2), No. 249 (2) P3576, P3616 (T10). **18 Aug:** No. 17 (2), No. 32 (3), No. 43 R4109, No. 85, No. 111 (3), No. 151 (2), No. 257 P3708, No. 501 (7), No. 504, No. 601 (2) L1990, No. 615 (11) L1592, P2768, P2966, R4221 (T37). **21 Aug:** No. 56 (1). **22 Aug:** No. 32 P3205 (T1). **23 Aug:** No. 85, No. 232 P3104 (2). **24 Aug:** No. 32 (5), No. 73, No. 151 (2), (8). **25 Aug:** No. 17 (2), No. 32 (2), No. 87, No. 213 (2),(T8). **26 Aug:** No. 1 (3), No. 56 (2), No. 85, No. 111, No. 310 (3), No. 615 (4) (T15). **27 Aug:** No. 213 (T1). **28 Aug:** No. 56 (4), No. 151, No. 610 (T6). **29 Aug:** No. 85 (3), No. 151, No. 501 (2) (T6). **30 Aug:** No. 43 (T2), No. 56, No. 85, No. 151 (2), No. 253 (3), (T9). **31 Aug:** No. 1 (4), No 56 (4), No. 85 (3), No. 111, No. 151, No. 253, No. 257 (2) R4903, No. 310 (2), No. 601 5) P5208, P3735, N2602, P3949, P3383 (T25).

1 Sept: No. 1 (4), No. 79 (3), No. 85 (4),(T13). **2 Sept:** No. 43 (3), No. 46 (2), No. 111 (2), No. 249 (2), No. 253 (3), V6640, P3610, No. 303, No. 501 (3) L1578, V7234 (T18). **3 Sept:** No. 1 (2) P3044, P3782, No. 17 (2), No. 46 (3), No. 238 R2680, No. 249, No. 253, No. 257 (2) L1703, P3578, No. 303, No. 310 (T13). **4 Sept:** No. 46 (3), No. 79, No. 111 (3), No. 253 V6638, No. 601 R4214 (T8). **5 Sept:** No. 73 (3), No. 79, No. 249 (2) No. 501 (T7), **6 Sept:** No. 73, No. 111 (2), No. 249, No. 253, No. 303 (6), No. 501 (3) V6612, V6646, P3516, No. 601 (4) V6647, P3382, P3363, P8818 (T22). **7 Sept:** No. 43 (2), No. 73, No. 79, No. 111, No. 242 (2), No. 249 (6) No. 257 (4) P3049, V7254, V7317, No. 303 (2), No. 504 (2) L1615, P3021 (T15). **8 Sept:** No. 46 (2), No. 605 L2061 (T3): **9 Sept:** No. 1, No. 242 (2), No. 303, No. 310 (2), No. 604 L2049, No. 605 P2765, No. 607 (6) (T14). **11 Sept:** No. 1 (2) V6670, No. 46 (3), No. 73, No. 213, No. 229 P3038, N2466 (2), No. 238 (3) P3096, V7420, R2682, No. 303 (2), No. 504 P3429 (T18). **14 Sept:** No. 73 (5), No. 253 (T7). **15 Sept:** No. 1 (3) P3080, P3876, L1973, No. 229 (2) V6616, N2537, No. 238 L1998, No. 242, No. 253, No. 303 (2), No. 310 (2), No. 501 (2) V7433, P2760, No. 504 (3) P2725, N2481, N2705, No. 604 L2012, No. 607 (T20). **16 Sept:** No. 605 P2589 (T1). **17 Sept:** No. 17, No. 501 (2), No. 504 P3383, No. 607 (2), (T7). **18 Sept:** No. 3 P3020, No. 25, No. 46 (2), No. 501 (2) V6600, V6620 (T4). **20 Sept:** No. 56 (T1). **23 Sept:** No. 73 (4) P8812, L2036, P3226, No. 229 N2879, No. 257 P3643 (T6). **24 Sept:** No. 17 (2), No. 151 (2) V7432, P3306, No. 601 R4120, No. 605 P3832, No. 615 (T6). **25 Sept:** No. 607 (T1). **26 Sept:** No. 238 (2) V6792, R4099, No. 303 (3), (T5). **27 Sept:** No. 229 (2) V6782, P3603, No. 242 P2967, No. 249 (3) V6729, P3834, V6622, No. 310, No. 501 (2) V6672, V6645 (T10). **28 Sept:** No. 238 (3) V3984, N2546, R3836, No. 249 V6617, No. 501 (3) V7497, P3417, P3605 No. 605 (2) P3828, V6699, No. 607 (2), (T12). **29 Sept:** No. 79 (3), No. 253 (2) V6621, No. 615 (T6). **30 Sept:** No. 56 (5) P2866, No. 229 (5) P3227, N2652, P2815, P3037, V6801, V6727, No. 302, No. 504 (2) P3021, 3414 (T13).

1 Oct: No. 238 (2) R4099, P3599, No. 248, No. 607 (2) (T4). **5 Oct:** No. 303, No. 607 (3) (T5). **6 Oct:** No. 64 P3716 (T1). **7 Oct**: No. 56 P3514, No. 238 V6799, No. 245 N2707, No. 501 (2) V6800, V6799, No. 605 (2) V7305, P3677, No. 607 (2) (T9). **8 Oct:** No. 229 V6820, No. 303, No. 312 (T3). **9 Oct:** No. 1 V7376 (T1). **10 Oct:** No. 56 P3421, No. 238 P3984, No. 249 V6878, No. 253 L1928, No. 312 L1547 (T5). **11 Oct:** No. 73, No. 249 V6728, No. 253 (2) V6570, L1666, No. 312 L1807 (T5). **12 Oct:** No. 145, P3896, V7426, No. 249 V6854, No. 257 (3) P3704, P3775, V7298, No. 605, P3302 (T8). **13 Oct:** No. 17 P3536 (T1). **14 Oct:** No. 605 P3107. **15 Oct:** No. 46 (3), No. 145 V7337, No. 213, No. 229 P3214, No. 229 P3456, No. 253 V6756, No. 257 V7351, No. 313 (2) V6846, V6811, No. 501 (2) V6722, P5194, No. 605 N2456 (T12). **18 Oct:** No. 145 V6856, No. 302, P3872, No. 302 (3) P3931, P3930, V6571 (T5). **19 Oct:** No. 3 P3260 (T1). **21 Oct:** No. 245 P3657 (T1). **22 Oct:** No. 257 (2) R4195, P2835, No. 605 V6783 (T3). **23 Oct:** No. 145 P3926 (T1). **24 Oct:** No. 43 V7307, No. 87, No. 111 P3046 (T3). **25 Oct:** No. 46, No. 79, No. 111 V6539, No. 151 L2047, No. 249 (2) V6958, V7409, No. 302 P3932, No. 501 (4) P2903, V6806, P5193, N2438 No. 601 (2) V6917, P3709 (T13). **26 Oct:** No. 151 (2) R4184, V7434, No. 229 (2) W6668, V6704, No. 605 V6943 (T7). **27 Oct:** No. 43 L1963, No. 145 (3) V7592 (T4). **29 Oct:** No. 1 (2) V7302, P5187, No. 46, No. 213, No. 232 V6848, No. 257 (2) V6852, P3893, No. 302 3085, No. 310, No. 615 (T8). **30 Oct:** No. 249 (T1).

Enemy aircraft known to have been destroyed by Hurricanes

Type	July	August	September	October	Total
Dornier Do 17	19	39	28	12	98
Heinkel He 111	17	42	35	15	109
Junkers Ju 88	10	21	-	10	32
Bf 109	15	105	101	42	119
Bf 110	12	75	58	11	263
Miscellaneous	8	7	3	4	22
Totals	**90**	**338**	**262**	**108**	**798**
Hurricanes lost	35	212	22	71	545

Hawker Hurricane Mk I with RAF Fighter Squadrons

Sqdn Codes	Period Service	1st Sttn.	CO (S Leader)
1 NA,JX	Oct 38-Jul 43	Tangmere, Sussex	I.A. Bertram
3 OP,QO	Mar 38-Apr 43	Kenley, Surrey	H.L.P. Lester
6 ZD,JV	Mar 41-Feb 42	Ramleh, M East	H.M. Massey
17 YB	Jun 39-Feb 41	Nth Weald, Essex	C. Walter
30 RS	Jun 41-Aug 42	Edku, Egypt	F.A. Marlow
32 GZ	Oct 38-Aug 42	Biggin Hill, Kent	R. Pyne
33 NW	Sep 40-Feb 42	Fuka, Egypt	C. Ryley
43 NQ,FT	Nov 38-Nov 42	Tangmere	R.E. Bain
46 PO	Mar 39-May 41	Digby	P.R. Barwell
56 US	Apr 38-Feb 41	Nth Weald	C.L. Lea-Cox
71 XR	Nov 40-May 41	Kirton in Lindsey	W.M. Churchill
73 TP	Jul 38-Jan 42	Digby	E.S. Finch
79 AL,NV	Nov 38-mid 41	Biggin Hill	G.D. Emms
80 AP	Jun 40-Jan 42	Amriya, Egypt	R.C. Jones
85 NO,VY	Sep 38-Apr 41	Debden, Essex	A.C.P. Carver
87 LK	Jul 38-Sep 42	Debden	J. Rhys-Jones
94 GO	May 41-Aug 42	Ismalia, Egypt	W.T.F. Wightman
111 TM,JU	Dec 37-Apr 41	Northolt, Middx	J.W. Gillan
121 AV	May 41-Jul 41	Kirton in Lindsey	K.J. Powell
127 BZ	Jne 41-Jne 42	Habbaniya, Egypt	J.M. Bodman
128 WG	Oct 41-Mar 43	Hastings, Sierra Leone	B. Drake
145 SO	Mar 40-Feb 41	Croydon, Surrey	J.D. Miller
151 GG,DZ	Dec 38-Jne 41	Nth Weald	E.M. Donaldson
181 EL	Sep 42-early 43	Duxford, Cambs	D. Crowley-Milling
183 HF	Nov 42-early 43	Church Fenton, Yorks	A.V. Gowers
185 GL	May 41-Jun 42	Hal Far, Malta	P.W. Mould
186 AP	Aug 43-Nov 43	Drem, Yorks	F.E.G. Hayter
213 AK	Jan 39-Mar 42	Wittering, Northants	J.H. Edwards-Jones
229 RE	Mar 40-May 41	Digby	H.J. Maguire

232 EF	Jul 40-Nov 41	Sumburgh, Orkney	Flt Lt M. Stephens
237 DV	Jan 42-Dec 42	Benghazi, Libya	E.T. Smith
238 VK	Jun 40-May 42	Middle Wallop, Hants	H.A. Fenton
242 LE	Feb 40-Apr 41	Church Fenton	F.M. Gobeil
245 DX	Mar 40-Aug 41	Leconfield, Yorks	E.A. Whiteley
247 HP	Dec 40-Jun 41	Roborough, Devon	P. St G. O'Brian
249 GN	May 40-May 42	Church Fenton	J. Grandy
250 LD	Feb 42-Apr 42	Gazala, Egypt	E.J. Morris
253 SW	Jan 40-Sep 41	Manston, Kent	E.D. Elliot
255 YD	Mar 41-Jul 41	Kirton in Lindsey	R. Smith
256 JT	Mar 41-Jul 41	Squires Gate, Lincs	G.H. Gathera
257 DT	Jun 40-Jul 42	Hendon, Middx	D.W. Bayne
258 ZT	Dec 40-Dec 43	Duxford	W.G. Clouston
260 HS	Dec 40-Feb 42	Castletown, IoM	W.B. Royce
261 -	Aug 40-Mar 42	Luqa, Malta	D.W. Balden
263 HE	Jun 40-Nov 40	Drem	H. Eeles
273 -	Aug 42-Dec 42	Katukurunda	A.N. Constantine
274 YK	Aug 40-Nov 41	Amriya, Egypt	P.H. Dunn
302 WX	Jul 40-Jul 41	Leconfield	W.A.J. Satchell
303 RF	Aug 40-Oct 41	Northolt	R.G. Kellett
306 UZ	Aug 40-Apr 41	Church Fenton	D.R. Scott
308 ZF	Nov 40-Apr 41	Baginton, Warwicks	Morris
310 NN	Jul 40-Mar 41	Duxford	G.D.M. Blackwood
312 DU	Aug 40-May 41	Duxford	F.H. Tyson
315PK	Feb 41-Jul 41	Acklington, Co Durham	H.D. Cooke
316 SZ	Feb 41-Aug 41	Pembrey, Carmarthen	J.A. Frey
317 JH	Feb 41-Jul 41	Acklington	C.J. Mount
331 FN	Jul 41-Aug 41	Catterick, Yorks	A.N. Cole
335 (FG)	Oct 41-Sep 42	Aqir, Palestine	X.J. Varvares
401 YO	Jun 40-Feb 41	Middle Wallop	E.A. McNab
402 AE	Dec 40-May 41	Digby	W.F. Hanna
450 -	May 41-Dec 41	Abu Sueir, Egypt	Flt Lt B. Shephard
488 -	Jan 42-Jan 42	Batavia, East Indies	J.N. McKenzie
501 ZH,SD	Mar 39-Apr 41	Filton, Bristol	M.V.M. Clube
504 AW,TM	Aug 39-Jul 41	Hucknall, Derby	H.M. Seeley
601 UF	Feb 40-Mar 41	Tangmere	L. Guiness
605 UP	Aug 39-Dec 40	Tangmere	Lord Willoughby
607 AF	Jun 40-Jun 41	Usworth, Co Durham	J.A. Vick
610 (JE)	Sep 39-Sep 39	Hooton Park, Cheshire	L.R. Parker
615 KW	Apr 40-Jul 41	Abbeville, France	J.R. Kayall
1435 Flt-	1941	Luqa, Malta	-

Enemy cannon fire damaged this aircraft's rear fuselage, but it only affected the fabric skin

The Hurricane airframe would absorb battle damage and still fly. Repairs on station were fairly simple.

V6586 Polish Squadron. 1940/41. Gloster-built, one of 1,700 examples.

Mk I, L1973, No. 1 Squadron, Tangemere. No. 3 Kenley, August 1939. RCAF, as JU-L, Northolt, September 1940. Damaged by a He111, South London, 15 September 1940.

Ten gun fighter/bomber with two 250lb bombs.

XR-J, No. 71 Eagle Squadron, V7608, November 1940.

Above left: *Damaged Hurricane of Belgium Air Force.* Above right: *Belgium Air Force Mk Is, damaged and abandoned by their own pilots. Wevelghem. Code 24/25, 1940.* Left: *Pilot Officer Nicholson VC. Wounded and on fire he turned his Hurricane behind an enemy aircraft and shot it down before abandoning his aircraft.*

Belgian Air Force Mk I, 1939/40.

Squadron Leader Tuck in his Mk I, Cotishall, January 1941. The flag is Burmese.

As seen on this Hurricane, the early aircraft of Fighter Command displayed black and white undersides.

CHAPTER SIX

Hurricanes Abroad

It is, perhaps, a little known fact that even at the height of the Battle of Britain Hurricanes were being sent overseas. Italy's entry into the war in June threatened to cut the British lifeline through the Mediterranean. At once plans were laid to fly Blenheims and Hurricanes direct to the Middle East, and in fact at least three such groups set out, refuelling in Southern France. One group, consisting of four Hurricanes and a Blenheim, arrived in Vichy France, where the Blenheim crashed. The Hurricanes, led by Flt Lt Barber, a South African, refuelled and flew to Tunisia. Landing beside a road and damaging a tailwheel in the process, the pilots refuelled once again and flew to Malta, where the aircraft later fought in defence of the island.

This 'direct' route proved too costly in aeroplanes, and eventually other routes and means were found to supply fighters to the Middle East, principally via Takoradi on the Gold Coast, but also by aircraft carrier to Malta. Meanwhile, the original tropical Hurricane, L1669, which had undergone trials at Khartoum before the war, was giving good service in the passive sense. Flown from airstrip to airstrip, it provided the illusion that the British air forces in Egypt were equipped with a number of Hurricanes, when in fact L1669 was alone and no longer able to fight!

By the end of 1940 Hurricanes were arriving in Egypt at a fairly steady rate, and three squadrons, Nos 73, 208 and 274, were fully equipped. Early arrivals had quickly succumbed to the desert grit, but new aircraft were fitted with Vokes air filters over their carburettor intakes. Long range fuel tanks were also introduced, particularly for the long African overland route, and for the small number of Hurricane Is modified in the field for reconnaissance duties.

One of the original 'Takoradi' Hurricanes, V7295, served as a prototype, being modified in December 1940 with a forward facing camera, in addition to a new engine. Termed the Tac R. Mark I, this was the first of about 200 such aircraft to be modified in the Middle East during 1941. They were issued to No. 208 (Army Co-operation) Squadron, No. 2 Photo-reconnaissance Unit and No. 680 (Photographic Reconnaissance) Squadron.

Some time later a number of these Hurricanes were fitted with Merlin XX engines to become Mark IIs, and were further modified with a fan of three, 8in or 14in oblique cameras in a ventral fairing. They were operated until mid-1942 throughout the Eastern Mediterranean theatre. A number of Hurricane Mark Is were used for night fighter defence of the Suez Canal during 1941. They were painted black overall and served with No. 212 Squadron.

Large numbers of Hurricanes served in the Middle East. This Mk I, No. 23 Squadron, is re-armed and re-fuelled at Famagusta airfield, Cyprus.

If air operations in Northern Europe during the winter of 1940/41 had settled into a pattern of German night attacks on British cities, and into a swing to the offensive by the RAF, events in the Mediterranean were moving swiftly following Italy's entry into the war. The successful resistance by Greece to Mussolini's attack through Albania turned to hard fought withdrawal in the face of German intervention. In January 1941 three Gladiator squadrons, Nos 33, 80 and 112, were ordered to Greece to reinforce the Greek Air Force against the *Regia Aeronautica*, although it was realised they would stand little chance in the event of *Luftwaffe* intervention. As stocks of Hurricanes in North Africa increased, the first Mark Is were ferried to Greece and issued to 'B' Flight, No. 80 Squadron, led by Flt Lt 'Pat' Pattle, a brilliant young South African who had already destroyed more than a dozen (and possibly a score of) Italian aircraft over Cyrenaica while flying Gladiators. The Hurricanes were soon in action and Pattle's score quickly mounted.

On 6 April German forces struck through Yugoslavia and within days were advancing against the Greek forces in the south. By the middle of the month most of the Gladiators in Greece had either been withdrawn or destroyed, and were being replaced by Hurricane Is.

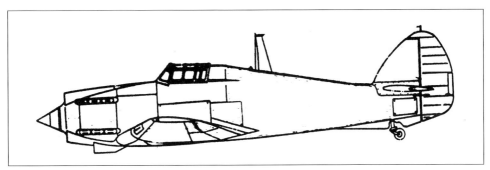

A possible shortage of Merlin engines during the Battle of Britain led to a trial installation of the Napier Dagger engine in a Hurricane Mk I. The fighter would have been slower than the Merlin-propelled version, but fast enough to cope with Luftwaffe *bombers.*

No. 208 Squadron, with Hurricanes and Lysanders, had also been sent to assist British forces, but it was already clear that evacuation was inevitable. Between 14 and 23 April about 26 Hurricanes, flying from Argos, Menidi and Paramythia, flew more than 300 sorties against the *Regia Aeronautica* and Luftwaffe, shooting down about 60 enemy aircraft (according to Italian and German records) and losing 22 of their own number. Pattle had been promoted to command No. 33 Squadron, shortly before he was shot down and killed over the sea off Megara. It has been suggested that at the time of his death his victory score had reached 40, a score that would put him at the top of the RAF list of Second World War fighter pilots. His actual score will never be known as it is clear that most RAF claims in Greece were not always supported, this is because the conditions in which RAF squadrons operated in this region were chaotic, to say the least. But it must be emphasised that Pattle's air combat was confined to a nine month period, most of which was spent flying and fighting in obsolete Gladiator biplanes.

After the fall of Greece the seven surviving Hurricane pilots were ordered back to Crete to cover the defence of the island against the anticipated invasion. They were joined by four Gladiators and three Fleet Air Arm Fulmars, most of which were destroyed at Maleme on the ground by enemy air attacks. Two Hurricanes were shot down over Suda Bay. A small number of replacement Hurricanes were sent out from Egypt, but by 19 May the air defence of the island rested on no more than four Hurricanes and three Gladiators, and it was decided to withdraw these survivors to Alexandria. In the German invasion that followed, the British forces, both on land and at sea, were at the mercy of almost unopposed enemy air attack and,

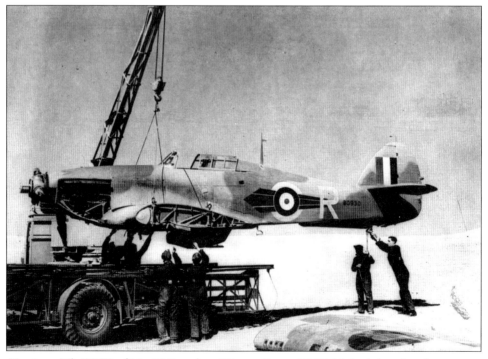

Hurricane Mk IIB(T) of No. 73 Squadron, Western Desert. BD930 is loaded up for salvage.

although the Hurricanes, flying from Egypt with 44 gallon drop tanks, did give some cover, they were operating at too long a range to offer more than a token protection.

As if to underline the justification of sending Hurricanes to the Middle East during the dark days of 1940, an abortive attempt by Rashid Ali to seize power in Iraq next demanded deployment of fighter strength at the RAF base at Habbaniya. In support of the Iraqi rebellion, the Germans sent a number of Bf110s and He111s, and these attempted not only to cover the Iraqi ground forces, but to bomb the base itself. No. 94 Squadron was sent from Egypt with a number of Gladiators and half a dozen tropicalised Hurricane Is and a single Tac R. Mark I. Ranging over Baghdad, Mosul and Erbil during May, these Hurricanes shot down enemy aircraft, probably about five, and lost two pilots. Most of these aircraft were equipped with 44 gallon drop tanks which, combined with the cumbersome desert air filter under the nose, reduced the Hurricane's top speed to about 240mph.

After the failure of Rashid Ali's forces to capture Habbaniya the Iraqi revolt collapsed and No. 94 Squadron returned to Egypt at the beginning of June. Meanwhile, other Hurricanes, flown by Nos 80, 208 and 260 Squadrons, had contributed to the successful elimination of Syria as a potentially hostile base which the Germans might have used against the Suez Canal. Indeed the Vichy Air Force Commander stated afterwards that it was the ability of the long range Hurricanes to strike the French base at Aleppo that contributed largely to his decision to surrender.

By the end of May 1941 the flow of Hurricanes to the Middle East was giving way to the Mark II, although Mark Is continued in front line service in North Africa for a further six months. Thereafter these veterans were relegated to a host of second line jobs, including weather reconnaissance throughout North Africa and elsewhere, operational training in Southern Africa, and patrols off the coast of Nigeria and the Gold Coast.

Hurricane Mk IIC(B)(T) with full load of 20mm cannon wing, plus two underwing bombs on strong points. Photographed in Burma. Cannons have anti-dust seals still in position.

Mk IIB, Z5227 of No. 81 Squadron, stationed at Vaenga, Russia, autumn 1941. Letters in grey, (code) numbers white as RAF identity.

Z3768, IIB, FK 49, 81 Squadron, Vaebga, Russia. Note bleak countryside.

Z5253, IIB, No. 134 Squadron, 151 Wing, Russia, Vaenga, Archangel, Russia.

Hurricane Mk I during the Finnish/Russia Continuation War. HLeLu 30 1942.

Yugoslavia Mk I in RAF camouflage, Langley.

Mk IV(T), No. 6 Squadron, Prkos airfield, Yugoslavia, May 1944. To Italy with eight Rps after 40mm anti-tank guns removed.

A poor-quality, but nevertheless interesting, photograph of French, Aeronavale, Hurricane, Paris 1945.

No. 306 Polish Squadron, Church Fenton. Merlin III engine.

Mk IIB(Trop), BD776, No. 128 Squadron, West Africa. Twelve gun wing.

L1669 was the first tropicalised Hurricane (Mk I). Despatched to Khartoum. Joined No. 80 Squadron, Helwan.

FAF Mk I, early 1942, as operated in the Russo-Finnish 'Continuation War'. HLeLv 30. Insignia under wings. Black/green camouflage. Yellow nose.

Mk IIB in red Air Force markings. Despatched from Middle East stocks.

Sea Hurricane Mk X, AM277 with twelve m/gns, was operated by US forces during 'Torch' landings in North Africa. This a/c was a Canadian built Mk X converted to Sea Hurricane Mk XIIB. St Leu, Algiers, 8 November 1942.

Two views of Persian Mk IIC Hurricane trainer. Above: *With no guns and RAF desert camouflage.* Below: *Dual seat version with four cannon wing.*

Canadian Sea Hurricane shot down near Oran, November 1942.

The Hurricane Mk X was the Canadian equivalent of the Mk I. Built by Cancar with twelve gun wing. AG162, EH-W.

Belgium Air Force Mk I with Rotol C/S prop, 1940.

Canadian Hurricane with Hamilton Standard propeller.

Hurricane Mk X, Fighter Leaders School. AG111.

Unusual leading edge ripple paint scheme.

Hurricane Mk I tests guns at butts at MU, Egypt.

Although Russia complained at the lack of aircraft from the Allies, large numbers were supplied, including Hurricane Mk IIB. This fighter was with the 72nd Regiment, Soviet Naval Air Fleet.

Hurricane Mk I during the Finnish/Russian Continuation War. HLeLv 30, 1942.

HU460 Mk I, HLeLv 30. Finnish Air Force.

Turkey operated the Hurricane. Illustrated is HV6-8, Mk IIC, one of twenty from ME RAF stock.

HL887, AK-W, Mk IV. No. 6 Squadron in Yugoslavia May 1944.

One of the few photos of Hurricanes in Malta.

Hurricane Mk I RAAF in Australian shadow shaded scheme.

Line up of Mk Is and IIs of No. 213 Squadron, Famagusta airfield, Cyprus, 1942.

Hurricane Mk I early production (tropical). P2627.

One of the few Hurricanes to sport squadron fuselage colours. P2638 of No. 208 Squadron, 285 Wing, Bing el Arat, 1942.

SAAF Hurricane of No. 1 Squadron, Sudan 1941.

Persian Air Force two seat trainer with Tempest canopy over rear cockpit.

Yugoslav Hurricane Mk IV

Belgian Air Force early Mk I Hurricane, winter 1939/40

A Canadian Hurricane X, AG122, used by Rolls-Royce for engine development

The first Yogoslav Hurricane Mk I, over Surrey. Note national markings on wings. Standard RAF day fighter camouflage.

A Canadian-built Hurricane, fitted with ski undercarriage and snowshoe tail component. It was intended to enable flying operations to continue unaffected by snow conditions in Canada.

Trials, Montreal, 1940. A Canadian-built Hurricane I (later to become Mk Xs).

This odd looking Hurricane had the Hillson upper (slip) wing. LI884 had the wing installed in Canada.

CHAPTER SEVEN

The War at Sea

The Sea Hurricanes

At the beginning of the Second World War the Royal Navy was poorly equipped with suitable aircraft. A series of Specifications issued on behalf of the Admiralty by the Air Ministry, had resulted in a series of indifferent, two-seat multi-purpose types. What the Navy lacked was an efficient fighter and it would feel this lack until variants of the Spitfire and Hurricane became available. The Spitfire was issued as Mark Is equipped with an arrester hook while it waited for a production aeroplane.

It was the Battle of the Atlantic that was to result in the Hurricane being adopted by the Navy and this situation came about when the Fw200 Condor, long range aircraft began attacking British shipping. A fighter was urgently needed and the Hurricane answered that need. The vessels from which the Hurricanes operated were the fighter catapult ships. A batch of Mark I Hurricanes were to be converted for catapulting on a rocket propelled sled.

As the Sea Hurricane Mark IA they were dispersed among the FASs and CAM (Catapult Aircraft Merchantman) ships. The Sea Hurricane was launched at 80mph. Following upon the success of the Mark IA the Air Ministry placed contracts for the Mark IB and a prototype, P5187, was ready for trials in March 1941. By the following October approximately 120 aircraft were ready but the Admiralty demanded a heavier armed aeroplane. As a result about 100 Mark IBs had four Oerlikon cannons installed and as such were designated the Mark IIC. It was intended that one or two of these camships would accompany each convoy and discharge their fighters on the appearance of an enemy aircraft. If out of range of land the Hurricane pilot would ditch his aeroplane into the path of the convoy in the hope that a ship would linger long enough to pick him up. In practice many pilots preferred to try to gain the mainland but often, sadly, were never seen again. The first camship to set sail was the *Michael E* on 27 May 1941, but she was torpedoed and sunk before launching her Hurricane. The first enemy to fall to a Hurricane was a Focke-Wulf Fw200, shot down by Lt R.W.H. Everett, RNVR, flying from HMS *Maplin* on 3 August that year, for which he was awarded the DSO.

During the first six months of the Second World War the fighter elements of the Fleet Air Arm possessed a motley collection of Gloster Sea Gladiators (top speed 250mph), Blackburn Skuas (225) and Rocs (223). Although flown with traditional courage and determination when the need arose, these aircraft were seldom a match for the modern aircraft of the *Luftwaffe*. Not even the Fairey Fulmar (272mph), which entered service during the Battle of Britain, gave much better promise. Indeed, it was the absence of

To combat the Fw200 Condor Atlantic raider the 'CAM' ship (Catapult Armed Merchant), Empire Tide, was introduced. These carried Hawker Hurricane Mk IAs readied for take-off on basic rocket catapult.

suitable British long range or naval fighters during the Norwegian campaign of 1940 that focused attention on the Hurricane's possible adaptation as a naval fighter.

After all, the RAF pilots of No. 46 Squadron, wholly untrained in carrier operations, had successfully taken off from the deck of HMS *Glorious*, and landed back on without the use of arrester gear. It was not as deck fighters, however, that the Hurricane first went to sea as a naval fighter. Towards the end of the Norwegian campaign Hawkers had planned to fit the floats of a Blackburn Roc to a Hurricane, but although a set of floats was fitted to a Hurricane wing centre section, the plan was abandoned before completion of a prototype.

Use of the camships was perceived as no more than an interim expedient, and the Sea Hurricane IA was intended primarily as a 'one shot' weapon, incapable of being retrieved at sea. Later, with the conversion of merchant ships to escort carriers, termed merchant aircraft carriers or MAC ships, Hurricanes were modified to incorporate deck arrester hooks under the rear fuselage, enabling them to land back on deck after a sortie. By the end of 1941 more than 200 of these hook-equipped Sea Hurricane IBs had been converted and were serving aboard HMS *Argus*, *Avenger*, *Eagle*, *Formidable*, *Furious* and *Victorious*.

Simultaneous with the introduction of the four cannon armed Hurricane Mark IIC, was the appearance of the Sea Hurricane IC, armed with four 20mm Hispano guns but

Sea Hurricane Mk IC.

still powered by the Merlin III. With deck hook fitted, this version possessed a top speed of slightly under 300mph at approximately 15,000ft. It entered service early in 1942 with Nos 801, 802, 803, 883, 885 and 889 Squadrons of the Fleet Air Arm, and went on to serve in almost every maritime theatre.

Operations by Sea Hurricanes during 1941 were almost entirely confined to CAM and MAC ships. However, in 1942, with fast increasing convoy activities, particularly in the North Atlantic following America's entry into the war, on the North Cape route to Russia and in the Mediterranean, Sea Hurricane ICs came to assume a vital role in the war at sea. Records suggest that by about June of 1942 the Fleet Air Arm possessed about 550 Sea Hurricanes Is, of which more than 200 were embarked at sea in various parts of the world.

When Japan entered the war in December 1941 there was not a single RAF Squadron east of India equipped with anything as modern as a Hurricane. Brewster Buffaloes of the RAF and Royal New Zealand Air Force constituted the sole fighter defence of the Malayan peninsula. Galvanised by the Japanese threat to Singapore, the Air Ministry ordered a shipment of fifty-one crated Hurricane Is and early Mark IIs to be diverted from the Middle East to Seletar, these aircraft, and twenty-four newly trained pilots, arriving safely at Singapore on 3 January 1942.

The Hurricanes were assembled during the following fortnight, the first eighteen being issued to Nos 232 and 488 Squadrons at Kallang to supplement the dwindling numbers of Buffaloes. Despite a conviction that these reinforcements would prove effective in stemming the Japanese, such was the extraordinary underestimate of enemy air supremacy, the Hurricane, severely handicapped by their desert air filters, proved little more successful against Japanese fighters than the Buffaloes. On 20 January Nos 232 and 488 Squadrons intercepted twenty-seven unescorted bombers over Singapore and shot down eight, losing three pilots.

The Japanese, obviously taken by surprise by the appearance of new fighters, returned the following day and on this occasion the Zero fighter escort destroyed five Hurricanes without loss. By the end of the month, after being employed in support of ground forces and as escort for elderly Vildebeest bombers, the Hurricane survivors had dwindled to

Mixed squadron of Mk I and Sea Hurricane Mk Is transferred to the Navy. Not navalised they were used for training only.

Sea Hurricane approaches for landing on carrier.

twenty, of which most were being flown by pilots of 232 Squadron. By 10 February only seven remained, and these were withdrawn to airfields near to Palembang on Sumatra. Thereafter such reinforcements that arrived in the East Indies, for instance No. 605 which flew off HMS *Indomitable*, were confined to Hurricane IIs, and it is believed that only one Hurricane Mark I survived to be withdrawn to Australia.

Elsewhere the Japanese opened their attack on Burma with an air raid on Rangoon on 23 December 1941 and met fighter defences composed solely of a handful of Buffaloes flown by No. 67 Squadron. As the invasion of South Burma developed in January 1942, the British diverted thirty Hurricane Is, being shipped to Singapore, to Burma and these were flown by pilots of the hastily formed No. 221 Group from airstrips at Mergui, Tavoy and Moulmein. Further reinforcements of Hurricane Is and early Mark IIs continued to arrive during February, but constant enemy raids and lack of spares reduced numbers to the point where, on 8 March, the day on which Rangoon fell to the Japanese, only five Hurricanes remained serviceable. From a study of surviving records, however, it is clear that the Hurricane pilots of 221 Group had, in six weeks, destroyed more than sixty Japanese aircraft. A further eighty falling to the guns of the Buffaloes and Curtiss P-40s of Colonel C.L. Chenault's American Volunteer Group.

Two further squadrons of mixed Hurricane Is and IIs arrived in Ceylon and these were deployed in Central Burma to cover the withdrawal of the British Commonwealth forces to Mandalay. By mid-1942 the only Hurricane reinforcements arriving in the Far East were Hurricane IIs, apart from Sea Hurricanes of the Fleet Air Arm, and by June that year all surviving Mark Is had been withdrawn to India and Ceylon.

Other Roles

Withdrawal of Hurricane Is from front line service in Europe in 1941, and elsewhere in

Sea Hurricane leaves light carrier deck with gun panels open.

With 'A' frame extended this Sea Hurricane Mk IB, M2-H, approaches to land.

1942, resulted in large numbers being returned to storage or relegated to second line duties. Nos 1412, 1413 and 1414 Meteorological Flights operated about a score of Mark Is on weather flights throughout the Middle East and North Africa during 1943 and 1944, while in India the last surviving 'Weather Hurricane' continued to fly until 1946. No. 116 (Calibration) Squadron was formed at Hendon in 1941, equipped with Hurricane Is, among other types, to fly calibration sorties for coastal radar and the Observer Corps. Another similar squadron, No. 527, was based at Hornchurch in 1943.

Several Hurricanes found their way into the Irish Air Corps. Three Mark Is force landed in Ireland (including P5176, built in Canada), but two of them were returned to the RAF in 1943. The following Mark Is were supplied under Contract. In all, fourteen carried Irish markings: 93 ex P5176, 94 ex Z2832, 95, 103, 104, 105 ex V7540, 106 ex Z4037, 107 ex P2968, 108 ex P3416, 109 ex V7173, 110 ex Z7158, 111, 112 and 114. A number remained in service until 1947.

In Africa about forty desert-weary Hurricane Is served with the Royal Egyptian Air Force during 1941-43, most of them being delivered to No. 1 (FR) Squadron at Cairo. With assistance from the RAF and the South African Air Force, some of them were kept in flying condition until shortly after the end of the war in Europe.

By the end of the war fewer than 200 Hurricanes remained airworthy throughout the world, and the majority of these were quickly allowed to disappear into the melting pots of peacetime salvage. Some museums were lucky enough to obtain examples for posterity, but by the early 1950s not one survived in a flyable condition. It was a sad end to the commentary on an aeroplane whose responsibilities had been of such a critical nature in those summer skies of 1940. Without the Hurricane the Battle of Britain could never have been fought, let alone won.

CHAPTER EIGHT

The Mark II Series

As the air armadas of *Luftwaffe* and Fighter Command clashed over the southern counties of England during the months from July to October 1940, shortcomings of the defending fighters in armament and performance were thrown into sharp relief. The Spitfire and Hurricane Mk I were successful in that the former could deal with enemy aircraft flying to 20,000ft plus, while the latter was in its element between 14,000 and 15,000ft. Their most formidable opponent was the Bf109, powered by the fuel injected Daimler-Benz 600 and armed with a mixture of a single 20mm cannon firing through the propeller hub and two MG 17 machine guns. It was faster but could be easily out-turned by both British fighters. What the Hurricane and Spitfire lacked was fire power. The eight Browning guns were lethal against the lightly armoured Heinkel III and Dornier 17 but the Bf109 carried sufficient armour to protect the vital areas of engine and cockpit.

Experiments taking place before the Battle of Britain started with Spitfires undergoing trials with two 20mm Hispano cannon mounted in the wings and the Hurricane mounting a pair of Oerlikons under the wings. Development of the Hurricane which was to eventually lead to the Mark II began in a desultory fashion in 1938 when early versions of the Mark I were being delivered to fighter squadrons of the RAF.

The standard engines for the Hurricane I were the Merlin II and III and on 6 July 1939 a Hurricane, L1856, was flown with the RM.3S, a Merlin III with a two-stage supercharger and de Havilland propeller. A second Mark I, L2026, had a Merlin XII installed for test, and flew on 13 July 1939. This engine was also installed in the Spitfire. Hurricane Mk I L1606 which had served with No. 56 Squadron before being seconded to the Hawker company, was used to flight test the Rolls-Royce RM.4S and Rotol 3-blade, constant speed propeller, making a first flight after modification on 9 June 1940. It then carried the civil marks G-AFKX. The Merlin RM.4S was rushed into production to power a batch of Spitfire Mk Is, and as the Merlin 45/46 series of engines was adopted as the power plant for the very successful Spitfire Mk V developed to combat the Bf109F.

A high altitude version of the Merlin engine, the Mark XX was also under development at the same period and had been specifically engineered for installation of a high altitude version of the Wellington bomber. It was also installed in a number of Spitfires. One of these high altitude engines, complete with Rotol RX.5/2 constant speed propeller, was delivered to the new Hawker factory at Langley, in Buckinghamshire, in April 1940, and conversion of a Mark I, P3269 commenced. It flew with the new power plant on 11 June 1940 and recorded a maximum speed of 348mph. A further batch of thirteen engines was delivered in June and the maximum speed of the Hurricane was increased to 348mph at 17,500 feet in S-gear.

Hurricane IIB, Z3661, with twelve .303in Brownings in wings. Additional guns outside landing lights.

However, the new Hurricane variant could not match the Spitfire at its best operating height.

The Air Ministry had anticipated the Hawker Hurricane Mark II with the placing of a contract, and under the full designation of Mark IIA Series I first models were in service with Fighter Command by September 1940, too late to have any major effect on the outcome of the Battle of Britain. In order to introduce the new variant into service as quickly as possible, a programme was initiated to convert a number of Mark Is to the improved standard in much the same manner that Spitfire Is were converted to accept the Merlin 45 to bring them up to Mk Vs. An initial test batch of approximately ten Hurricane Is was modified, and was followed by a second, larger, batch of forty. Even though there was a shortage in the RAF a number of the converted airframes were delivered to Russia despite a plea that Spitfires would have been more acceptable.

As mentioned above additional gun combinations were also under consideration, including the somewhat unreliable 20mm cannon, produced by the Hispano and Oerlikon companies. An Air Ministry Specification, F.37/35, of 28 March 1936, called for a single seat day and night fighter with an armament of not less than four 20mm cannon. The favoured guns were the Hispano and Oerlikon but the Vickers 12.7mm and 25.4mm were on offer as was the Vickers 'S', a 40mm weapon. Both Supermarine and Hawker submitted tenders using the basic Spitfire and Hurricane airframe as a gun platform utilising the Hispano and Oerlikon cannon. However, a third contender, Westland, was awarded the contract which resulted in production of the Whirlwind, twin Peregrine fighter. The concept was ideal; fast, heavily armed and twin engines for a margin of safety. However, the engine was faulty and the production programme floundered as engine problems delayed delivery and development.

In pursuit of its aim to prove to the Air Ministry that a single-engined aeroplane was more suitable to the demands of the F.37/35 Specification, Hawker installed a pair of Oerlikons under the wings of L1750 in 1938, but the Air Ministry was more concerned with production of the Hurricane to meet the most obvious threat from Germany, and the aeroplane was seconded for armament proving tests as part of the Whirlwind programme. The modified Hurricane flew for the first time on 24 May 1939.

Hawker re-submitted their cannon armed Hurricane in May 1940, this time with four Oerlikons installed in the wings, and had also, in the preceding January, suggested that a twelve Browning, metal wing version would be just as suitable. But, Fighter Command needed replacements to offset the losses suffered during the Battle for France and the proposal for shelved. However, the company did receive a single contract to modify a pair of wings taken from a war weary Hurricane I to take four Oerlikons. When an official from the Air Ministry inspected the installation, and considered the proposal, permission was given to install the new wings on a Mark I.

P2640 was chosen and it was flown for the first time on 7 June. There was a huge speed penalty due to the additional weight and drag (approximately 290mph at operational height), but the potential was recognised with the availability of the Merlin XX engine. The Hurricane was delivered to No. 151 Squadron on 19 August 1940 and trials took place while flying from North Weald. Encouraged by results three more Mark Is, V7260, V7360 and W9324, were modified They were sent to Boscombe Down for trials where the official Aero Reports referred to them as Hurricane Mark IICs. By this time the Battle of Britain had passed through its critical stages; a version of the Spitfire, the IIB, with twin Hispanos was into its service test programme with No. 19 Squadron, and there were insufficient numbers of the Merlin XX available to justify their installation in the Hurricane.

It was not until February 1941 that sufficient Merlin XXs reached Hawker, to be

Flight of No. 3 Squadron's Mk IICs armed with four wing cannon.

Mk IIB, BE417, Hurribomber, No. 402 Squadron, Rochford. Twelve guns and wing bombs (two at 250lb). AE-K, November 1941.

installed in V2461, Z2588, Z2885 and Z2891. They were considered to be prototype airframes for the forthcoming Hurricane Mark IIC. Two types of cannon were installed, the Oerlikon and Hispano. The new engine resulted in an increase of maximum speed to 336mph, and with the Vokes tropical filter this dropped to 320. The RAF declined initially to accept this mark with the Merlin III, but the Royal Navy had large numbers delivered beginning with Contract No. 62305/39. All had the Merlin XX engine and were delivered between January and July 1941, the first being delivered to No. 3 Squadron.

The Hawker design office was constantly producing proposals for improved versions of the Hurricane, and one result was the Mk IIA Series 2 with a 'universal' wing that had the following advantages – accommodation for eight or twelve Browning guns; strong points under the wings for ordnance or additional fuel tanks. The twelve gun wing was eventually introduced on the Langley production lines in late November 1940 to become the Mk IIB, prototype of which was Z2326, flight tested at Boscombe Down on 18 April 1941. The same aeroplane had strengthened wings for carriage of two 500lb GP bombs.

A tropicalised version of the IIB was tested on Z7480, a modified Mk IIA Series 2, test flown on 8 February 1941. First production example was AP516 from the Austin Motors line. The PR Mk IIB was used in the desert as an unarmed reconnaissance variant.

The Mark IIC

A grand total of 4,711 Mark IICs were delivered and produced at Langley, Gloster, Austin Motors and in Canada by the Canadian Car and Foundry Company. A number were converted from Mark IIA and IIBs and had four 20mm Oerlikon or Hispano cannon installed. The first Hurricane modified for the cannon wing was a Mk I, L1759 after trials had been conducted with two obsolete wings in February 1940.

Long range version of Hurricane IIC with full chord, 90gal overload tanks.

The first production four cannon (Merlin XX) Hurricane was V3760, flown during July 1940 and delivered for further trials to Boscombe Down on 5 December 1940. It was delivered to No. 151 Squadron for service trials. Early production models featured a belt fed Oerlikon, but this was speedily replaced by the standard drum. The new variant was introduced into RAF service in June 1941, and used in the many offensive sweeps over the Continent in the ground attack role. For this the Hurricane could be modified to carry two 250lb bombs under the wings. With this ordnance load and four cannon, performance suffered with maximum speed reduced to 220mph. Without the ordnance the tropical version, Mk IIC(Trop) would attain a maximum speed of 320mph.

Losses mounted and the Hurricane IIC was switched to a night fighter role by the autumn of the year. It was fitted with the AI Mark V radar in a container under one wing plus a 44gal overload fuel tank on the other. The radar aerials were located on the outer wing panels.

Despite their shortcomings the IIB and IIC were standard equipment for fifty-seven squadrons. A number of these specialised in the night intruder role, that of patrolling near the *Luftwaffe* night bombing bases and attacking the home coming bombers. Large numbers of IICs were used for the ill-fated Dieppe landings of 19 August 1942, when the Allies probed the strength of the German defences. A number of Turbinelite squadrons used the IIC as the attacking aeroplane accompanying the Havocs equipped with the nose mounted searchlight when seeking out the German night raiders. A total of sixteen Hurricane squadrons were eventually deployed against the German night bombers. In the period when Allied air forces were softening up Northern France in anticipation of the D-Day landings, IICs were in the forefront of the ground attack squadrons. They were equipped with rockets, anti-personnel bombs, and the SCI smoke containers to cloak amphibious landings by commandos probing the defences.

Where the IIC was most heavily involved was the Middle and Far East theatres. A contract

Mk IIB Hurribomber, No. 402 Squadron, RCAF, Warmwell. AE-W, December 1941. Also, No. 715 Squadron, March 1942.

had been placed for 300 examples with the Austin Motor Company, fitted with the 'Universal' wing. Hawker Aircraft had also developed the Mk II, Series 2 which could be fitted with either an eight or twelve gun armament. A small, experimental batch had an additional bay of 6.5in inserted in front of the cockpit, but when flown with a Vokes tropical filter the aeroplane suffered from instability. The IIA and IIBs started arriving in the Canal Zone in the summer of 1941, and the immediate result was the failure of the Merlin XX due to ingestion of sand.

The cumbersome Vokes was installed but this was to restrict performance to such an extent that the fighter was handicapped when meeting its old enemy, the Bf109. In an attempt to boost performance the number of guns was reduced to two. No attempt was made to install the local modification, desert, filter (Aboukir) as fitted to the Spitfire. Reinforcements continued to pour in and by November the same year no less than forty RAF squadrons had the Mark II on strength.

The Middle East Air Force needed a reconnaissance aeroplane and while awaiting delivery of the Spitfire PR IV a number of Hurricanes were modified to carry vertical and oblique cameras. With guns removed they were re-designated PR Mk II. The TAC R, built on the

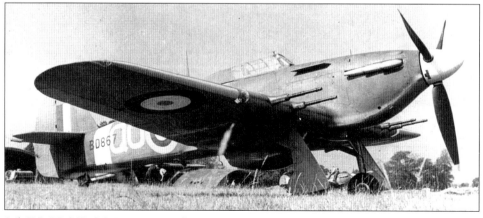

Mk IIC, BD867, QO-Y. No. 3 Squadron. Four 20mm cannon. Offensive daylight sweeps, France 1941.

production lines followed. Prototype PR Hurricane was DG613/G, a 'guard' aeroplane, and was converted at Heliopolis in May 1941. It was to be used for tactical reconnaissance and equipped with a forward facing F.24. The normal Mark IIA, B or C armament was carried. The TAC.R had two oblique F.24, 8in lenses in a ventral, rear fuselage, fairing, and all armament was removed. For high altitude work two oblique and one vertical, all with 14in lenses, were positioned in the rear fuselage and it lacked armament. Other Hurricanes were employed in the meteorological role. The IIC fought in the *Torch* landings in French Algeria and Morocco, and when Sicily was invaded in preparation for the assault on the Italian mainland thirteen Hurricane squadrons were available. A surprise user of the Hurricane was the US Navy. They had acquired a number of Canadian-built Sea Hurricanes, Mark Xs converted to IIC, and they were to be used, albeit in small numbers, in the same campaigns.

In the Far East campaign the Hurricane was a welcome sight to servicemen after months of waiting for a modern interceptor with which to beat off the Japanese air onslaught. The first IICs arrived in India and Ceylon in 1942, and as supplies built up a total of sixteen squadrons was serving in North Burma, India and Ceylon; 670 were based in India and 200 of these were seconded to the Indian Air Force. Two years later the total had grown and twenty-nine squadrons equipped. Russia demanded supplies of aeroplanes from the Allies, and the need for fighters was satisfied with Spitfires, P-40s and Hurricanes. The first reached Russia in August 1941 as part of a unit consisting of Nos 81 and 134 Squadrons complete with RAF crews. After withdrawal of the RAF contingent the Hurricanes were left to the Russians. Cannon armed IICs were delivered via the Middle East. Other air forces, such as Portugal, Persia and Eire, took delivery of the Hurricane IIC, albeit that the latter was equipped with Hurricanes that had force landed.

Extending the Range

Like its contemporary, the Spitfire, Camm's Hurricane was the vehicle for numerous trials and

Mk IIC 'Nightingale', No. 87 Squadron, night fighter. Charmy Down, September 1942. HL864. Long range fuel tanks.

experiments. Both fighters had been designed from the outset as Metropolitan Interceptors, as it had been calculated that from the moment an enemy aeroplane had been plotted by sound (this was before the advent of radar) the Metropolitan Fighter would have just three minutes to take off from a forward airfield, climb and meet that enemy before it had located its intended target and released the bomb load. Hence the requirement for a heavily armed, lightweight interceptor with a minimal combat radius. The Battle of Britain demonstrated the sound reasoning of planners. However, when that same fighter was required to carry the air war to the *Luftwaffe* based in France, its limited range was to prove an embarrassment.

When the fighter sweeps were launched against enemy installations on the Continent pilots discovered, as did their contemporaries in the *Luftwaffe*, that there was a limited time in which they could concentrate on ground strafing and engage the enemy aircraft after making allowance for the Channel crossing. Additional fuel was an urgent necessity and the overload fuel tank developed from the 30gal slipper to the huge 170 or 200 gal ferry tanks. The latter were needed when reinforcement aeroplanes were flown to Gibraltar, Malta and the Middle East.

The ferry problem was grappled in several ways – one bizarre proposal was to mount, in pack-a-back fashion, a fighter on the backs of war weary bombers such as the Wellington and Whitley. These same bombers were to be adapted as tugs, towing fighters by means of cables attached to rear fuselage positions. A third scheme was termed 'Hasty Hitch' which involved British fighters towing a Hotspur glider carrying ground crew and other personnel to forward airfields as the Allied advanced in Normandy. The tow line was attached to the fighter's tail wheel and dropped when the two aeroplanes had reached the destination.

Armament

A ten and twelve Browning gun armament was developed for the Hurricane. The former was rarely installed; the latter was a development from the Tornado design programme. The two Hurricane developments could also carry bombs – 250 and 500lbs – rockets, and large calibre, slow firing guns at an increased gross weight. In 1941 a programme was launched to develop

Mk IIC, No. 87 Squadron, during service and loading of 20mm cannon.

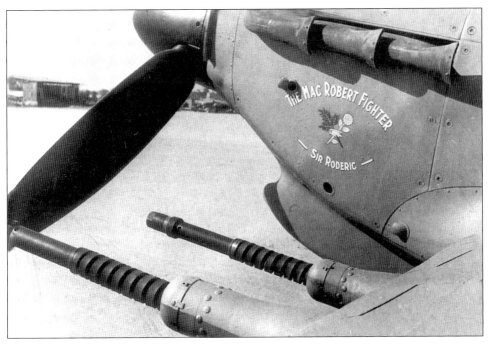

Hurricane with four 20mm cannon.

rocket projectiles, crude objects initially consisting of a length of 3in piping filled with a propellant, plus an explosive head and tail fins. The first Hurricane used for rocket trials was Z2415, a Mk IIA Series with three launch rails under each wing. The 60lb head caused great damage when a direct hit was registered, and when a cluster found its target the danger was multiplied. The number of RPs was increased to eight and the ripple salvo developed.

The 20mm cannon was a successful development, but in the preparation for Alamein and, later, Normandy landings, the development of a large calibre gun was required. One already existed, the Vickers 'S' gun of 40mm calibre. Also under development, but much later, was the Rolls-Royce BF (Belt Fed). The 'S' gun was undergoing trials in the Vickers Wellington with a trial installation of one, or two, mounted in the nose position. This armament was considered to be ideal for anti-shipping strikes. A Wellington was also fitted with the gun in a specially developed dorsal turret.

The anti-tank Mk IID

The Hurricane was considered to be an ideal mount for an anti-tank gun and the 'S' was installed under the wings. The first Hurricane to have the gun installed was a Mark II Z2326 with strengthened wing. Its maiden flight was on 18 September 1941, and it was despatched to Boscombe Down for proving tests. After a short stay at Farnborough the Hurricane was returned to Langley and a pair of Rolls-Royce guns installed in place of the 'S'. However, it was not as reliable as the 'S', which had been under development for a long period, and it only carried twelve, as compared with the fifteen rounds of the 'S'.

4 production examples were used for exhaustive trials and with the 'S' gun installation the Hurricane was known as the Mark IID. The first 92 examples were delivered to the RAF in February 1942 with two .303in Brownings in the wings. A total of approximately 800 IIDs were constructed, all on the normal production line, and the majority were sent to the Middle East to take part in the great tank battles of the desert. After the desert campaign was completed with Rommel's defeat, large numbers of IIDs were sent to Russia.

There was a final variant, the IIE, development of which started in March 1942. The various modifications to the original wing design caused problems, as did the requirements for close support and ground attack modifications.

Frontal armour to include protection of the radiator was required, and as the prototype neared completion during January 1943 a new engine was proposed, the Merlin 32 low altitude variant. Increased armament, modified wings and fuselage, all increased weight and Hawker considered that a new designation would be more applicable than designating it as a sub variant of an existing Mark, i.e. the Mk II. An interesting experiment was a series of trials with IIDs having asymmetric wing loads of one 40mm gun under one wing, plus four 3in rockets under the other.

It was agreed and the new Hurricane was to become the Mk IV. During the same period Hawker had been producing proposals for Hurricanes with more powerful engines, armament and strengthened airframe. One of these was the projected Mk III. This was viewed as a sub variant of the Mk IIE with the Packard-Merlin 24, 27 or 28 with the universal wing capable of carrying (1) 20mm anti-tank guns (2) rocket projectiles (3) various weight bombs and (4) additional, long range fuel tanks. There was also a suggestion that future variants of the Hurricane and Spitfire could use the same basic external and internal equipment such as propellers, radios, armament.

The Hurricane Mk II with two 40mm Vickers 'S' guns.

Mk IIC, LB836, ninth production batch of 1,205 examples, 1943.

Hurricane IIB fighter bomber with two 250lb bombs on panniers.

Leading Particulars Mark II Series

Wing span: 40ft 0in. *Length:* 32ft 2.5in. *Height:* tail down, 13ft 1in. *Gross wing area:* 257.6sqft. *Aspect ratio:* 6:2. *Wing incidence to dataum:* +2°. *Dihedral:* 3.5°. *Root chord:* 8ft 1in. *Tip:* 3ft 11.25in. *Wing loading:* 22lb/sqft. *Power loading:* 5.5lb/hp. *Tailplane span:* 11ft 0in. *Undercarriage track:* 7ft 7in. *Powerplant:* Rolls-Royce Merlin XX of 1,260hp @ 3,000rpm @ 11,750 feet, MS gear; 1,160hp @ 3,000rpm @ 20,750 feet, S gear; take off (at S/L) 1,300hp @ 3,000rpm. *Propeller/s:* Rotol RS.5/2, 3-blade (Schwarz) and/or Rotol RS.5/3 with Jablo blades. *Diameter:* 11ft 3in.

Weight:

IIB Tare 5,467lb, gross 7,233lb. **IIB(T)** Tare 5,594lb, gross 7,396lb. *Maximum overload:* 7,896lb. **IIC** Tare 5,658lb, gross 7,544lb. *Overload:* 8,044lb. **Tropical** Tare 5,785lb, gross 7,544lb. *Overload:* 8,207lb. **IIC(T)** Tare 5,785lb, gross 7,707lb. *Maximum overload:* 8,207. **IID(T)** Tare 5,550lb, gross 7,850lb. **Sea Hurricane IIC** Tare 5,708lb, gross 7,618lb. **Sea Hurricane IIC(T)** Tare 5,708lb, gross 8,278lb.

Performance:

Mk IIA Series 2 (clean) *Speed:* 272mph @ S/L, 287mph @ 5,000ft, 304mph @ 10,000ft, 332mph @ 25,000ft. *Max speed:* 342 @ 17,500ft. *Rate of climb:* 5000ft in 2.1min; 10,000ft in 3.8min; 25,000ft in 12.4min; *Time to height:* 23.2min to 35,000ft. *Range:* 460 miles @ 178mph, with two 44gal overload tanks 920 miles. *Ceiling:* 36,300ft.

Mk IIA (Trop) Series 2 *Speed:* 265mph @ S/L; 280mph @ 5,000ft; 296mph @ 10,000ft; 324mph @ 25,000. *Max speed:* 334mph @ 17,5000ft. *Rate of climb:* 2,800ft/min @ S/L; 2,480ft/min @ 5,000ft; 2,150ft/min @ 10,000ft; 1,120ft/min @ 25,000ft. *Time to height:* 25.4min to 35,000ft. *Ceiling:* 34,000ft.

Mk IIA, Series 2 Ordnance carried *Speed:* 247mph @ S/L; 258mph @ 5,000ft; 268mph @ 10,000ft; 280mph @ 25,000ft. *Max speed:* 308mph @ 17,500ft. *Rate of climb:* 2,200ft/min @ S/L; *Time to height:* 4.6min to 5,000ft; 9.1min to 10,000ft; 24.9min to 25,000ft. *Ceiling:* 27,000ft.

Mk IIB (clean) *Speed:* 256mph @ S/L; 280mph @ 5,000ft; 295mph @ 10,000ft. *Max speed:* 330mph @ 17,800ft. *Rate of climb:* 2,960ft/min @ S/L; 2,800ft/min @ 5,000ft; 2,390ft/min @ 10,000ft; 1,350ft/min @ 25,000ft. *Time to height:* 21min to 35,000ft. *Ceiling:* 36,000ft.

Mk IIB with bombs *Speed:* 217mph @ S/L; 237mph @ 5,000ft; 260mph @ 10,000ft; 270mph @ 25,000ft. *Max speed:* 287mph @ 17,800ft. *Rate of climb:* 2,830ft/min @ S/L; 2,500ft/min @ 5,000ft; 2,100ft/min @ 10,000ft; 1,150ft/min @ 25,000ft. *Time to height:* 24.9min to 35,000ft. *Ceiling:* 35,600ft.

Mk IIB (Trop) bombs *Speed:* 200mph @ S/L; 217mph @ 5,000ft; 227mph @ 10,000ft; 226mph @ 25,000ft. *Max speed:* 246mph @ 17,800ft. *Rate of climb:* 2,410ft/min @ S/L; 2,190ft/min @ 5,000ft; 1,750ft/min @ 10,000ft. *Ceiling:* 29,900ft.

Mk IIC (clean) *Speed:* 260mph @ 5,000ft; 279mph @ 10,000ft; 290mph @ 25,000ft. *Max speed:* 329mph @ 17,800ft. *Time to height:* 1.7min to 5,000; 3.4min to 10,000ft; 10.1min to 25,000ft; 24.6min to 35,000ft. *Ceiling:* 35,600ft.

Mk IIC(Trop) bombs *Speed:* 203mph @ S/L; 223mph @ 5,000ft; 241mph @ 10,000ft; 208mph @ 25,000ft. *Max speed:* 275mph @ 17,800ft. *Rate of climb:* 2,280ft/min @ S/L; 1,930ft/min @ 5,000ft; 1,600ft/min @ 10,000ft; 1,210ft/min @ 25,000ft. *Ceiling:* 30,800ft.

Sea Hurricane Mk IIC *Speed:* 260mph @ S/L; 275mph @ 5,000ft; 286mph @ 10,000ft; 307mph @ 25,000ft. *Max speed:* 317mph @ 17,500ft. *Rate of climb:* 2,010ft/min @ S/L; 1,760ft/min @ 5,000ft; 1,520ft/min @ 10,000ft; 610ft/min @ 25,000ft. *Ceiling:* 30,800ft.

Armament: four 20mm Hispano or Oerlikon cannon with 364 rounds.

Mk IIAs, No. 1423 Flight, Kaldanes Airfield, Iceland, early 1941. Squadron formed from No. 98 Bomber Squadron. Note non-standard leading edges

Line up of No. 164 Squadron Mk IICs armed with anti-tank Vickers 'S' guns. Middle Wallop, June 1943. KX413 nearest camera.

Hurricane Mk IIC Night Fighter armed with four 20mm Hispano cannon. Note anti-glare strake ahead of cockpit to counter exhaust flames.

Hurricane Mk IIC, LF380 of No. 83 OTU. Then No. 1636 Bomber Defence Training Flight, June 1944.

This Hurricane Mk II, Z2515, was used for engine-airscrew compatibility trials at Boscombe Down.

A twelve-gun fighter, the Hurricane Mk IIB.

A Hurricane IIC, at Brooklands in 1942, fitted with 44-gallon long-range fuel tanks.

A Hurricane IIC, at Langley, with 90-gallon ferry fuel tanks.

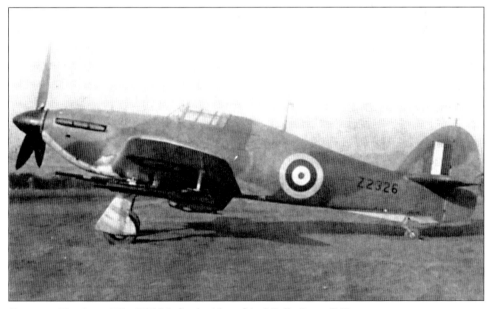

Prototype Hurricane IID, Z2326, fitted with unfaired Rolls-Royce B.F. guns.

Hurricane IID, KZ320, armed with Vickers 40-mm anti-tank guns.

Two views of a tropical Photo Reconnaissance (PR) Hurricane Mk IIC.

The first rocket-equipped Hurricane, Z2415, fitted with three rails under each wing. Boscombe Down, 1942.

Plan view of Mk IV with Vickers 'S' guns.

CHAPTER NINE

Mark IV and V Series

The logical successor to the Mark II Series should have been the Mark III, if the normal procedure for designating had been followed, but during the period when many improvements were being made to the basic airframe a host of projects were either under consideration or in the process of evolution. In 1941 new weapons were coming on stream and a number of aircraft were used for proving tests, among them the Hurricane. At around the period that the 'universal wing' was developed for both the Spitfire and Hurricane, the RP, rocket projectile, was under consideration as an attack weapon in addition to the normal machine gun or cannons of the two fighters. A two Browning gun version was considered but rejected.

The development of the British fighter with an all purpose 'universal wing' was promoted in late 1940 with, in the instance of the Hurricane, the Hurricane IIA with Merlin XX engine, eight to twelve gun wing and shackles for bombs, rockets, drop and ferry fuel tanks, and Air Ministry permission was granted.

The new variant was projected as the Mk IIE with the Universal wing, that could also be adopted to carry anti-tank guns, such as the 40mm cannon. At the same period of time Rolls-Royce had developed the Merlin 27 with 1,280hp.

All activity on the IIE ceased and work started on a new prototype when a Mk II production Hurricane (KX405) was converted to accept a Merlin 45 engine. It was tropicalised, fitted with two Vickers 'S' 40mm cannon in under wing housings, deepened radiator and extra armour, and designated as the Hurricane Mk IV.

A Hurricane IIA Series 2, Z2415, also fitted with a 'universal wing', had three RP launch rails installed under each wing and, to add to its suitability to act as a trials aircraft, it also possessed strengthened wing spars. Z2415 was delivered to Boscombe Down in March 1942. Two further Mark IIAs were ready for trials later in the year. The trials were successful in that although the RPs were not 100% accurate, a salvo of eight, later to become standard complement, provided sufficient spread to guarantee a strike.

Development of Z2415 and its companions was shelved but in the final months of 1941 Rolls-Royce offered the Air Ministry a Merlin engine with a longer life between services, and Hawker began initial design of the Mark IIE, which would incorporate a 'universal wing', plus provision for RPs and the 40mm cannon from Vickers and Rolls-Royce. It was viewed as a middle altitude aeroplane, operating at advantage at around 14,000 feet. However, official interest waned and a new variant was offered.

This Hurricane would use the Merlin 32, low altitude engine, with a 4-blade Rotol propeller. A single prototype, KX405, was prepared and immediately fitted with twin Vickers 'S' guns. Although part of a contract for 1,200 Hurricanes IIB, C and D, and

Hurricane KX405 Mk IV(T) during trials. It was converted at a later stage to Mk IV standards.

intended as a 'D', KX405 was to make its maiden flight as the Mark IV on 14 March 1943. It bore this designation for a very short time as it was finally converted to fly as the Mark V prototype, still with the Merlin 32. To add to its convoluted life it was to go through a third metamorphosis to become a standard Mark IV. A second Hurricane, KZ193, flew as a Mark V prototype but had the 3-blade Rotol. It, too, was converted to Mark IV standard and was delivered to No. 164 squadron with 40mm guns and used for anti-shipping patrol.

The Mark IV entered production but was delivered to the RAF on a restricted basis. It could carry either 250 or 500lb bombs under the wings, between two to eight clusters of RPs or 40mm guns. A total of 524 Mark IVs were constructed and operated in all war theatres.

Hurricane Mark V

The Hurricane Mark V prototype, KX405 was to be much improved after conversion from a Mark IV to the Mark V. It retained the Merlin 32 and Rotol propeller, and this engine could be 'ground-boosted' and run on 150 octane fuel, code name 'Basta'. It reached 326mph at very low level and showed its great promise as a ground attack weapon. A second Hurricane, NL255, a single aeroplane constructed to a special contract, flew in late 1943 but it was the sole representative of the final Mark for all development work and a production contract were cancelled.

Without the Hurricane the outcome of the Battle of Britain would most certainly have been different to the famous victory won by 'the few'. It operated on all continents and endeared itself to the thousands of pilots who flew it. Interceptor, ground attack fighter, anti-tank and anti-shipping weapon, night fighter. It performed all roles with élan and although not as glamorous as its companion of those desperate months of summer 1940, it, too, will be long remembered with gratitude and fond memories by a generation that fought the Second World War.

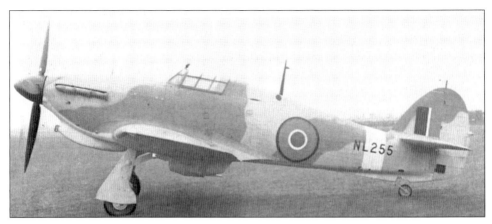

The second Hurricane V prototype, NL255.

Hurricane Variants

F.36/34 prototype, K5083. 'Interceptor Monoplane', with 1,025hp Merlin C. Eight .303in m/gns in wings. First flight 6 November 1935.

Mk I. First production examples, 1,030hp Merlin II/III. Armament as K5083. Fabric wings on early models, metal later.

Mk I Tac R. Middle and Far East examples modified for Tactical Reconnaissance duties.

PR Mk I. Fighter with armament deleted and additional fuel and cameras.

Mk IIA Series 1. Merlin XX of 1,185hp, two stage supercharged engine. Eight .303s.

Mk IIA Series 2. Universal wing introduced.

Mk IIB. Universal wing with twelve .303s, wing shackles for fuel tanks, 250 or 500lb bombs.

TacR Mk IIB. Tactical reconnaissance in desert. Forward facing F-24 or cine camera in starboard wing root or two oblique F-24 (8in lens) in rear fuselage. Total of 194gals fuel.

Mk IIB. Hurribomber. Ground attack and close support variant, Desert/Far East. Also Coastal Patrol.

Mk IIC. Major model. Universal wing with four 20mm cannon, wing shackles for fuel tanks and bombs. Large numbers with tropical fliters. Intruder ops.

TacR Mk IIC. Tactical reconnaissance

Mk IID. Multi-role/gun variant with two 40mm Vickers S (15rpg) or Rolls-Royce (12rpg), anti-tank/ship/armoured vehicle variant. Secondary armament of twin .303s in wing. Additional armour around engine and cockpit. Shackles for bombs and fuel tanks. Desmo car mirror fitted by pilots.

Mk II. Lightweight version for high altitude defence of Suez Canal zone.

Mk II. Met. Weather investigation type.

PR Mk II. Primarily for reconnaissance in Middle East.

Mk II. Hurribomber. Ground attack, support version used in India, Burma and convoy escort.

Mk IIE. Design only but later redesignated as Mk IV.

Mk III. Variant scheduled for the Packard-Merlin 28. Three prototypes only and became prototype Mk V.

Mk IV. Packard-Merlin 24.27 of 1,280hp. Universal wing. Armament of six/eight 3in rockets, or Long Tom single. Drop fuel tanks, bombs, anti-tank 40mm guns. Trop variant also.

Mk V. Mark IV, KZ193 converted with Merlin 27 engine rated at 1,700hp. and 4-blade prop of 10ft 9in dia. Anti-tank guns, ground boosted engine. Two prototypes only (plus Mk III) and no production.

Mk X. Originally Canadian built version of Mk I with Packard-Merlin 28. 100 with eight .303s and majority with twelve .303s or four cannon metal wings.

Mk XI. Total of 150 built by Cancar originally with eight guns. Many converted with twelve gun and four cannon wings.

Mk XII. Total of 248 with twelve .303s, later examples had four cannon.

Mk XIIA. 150 with Packard-Merlin, 29 with 3-blade Hamilton Hydromatic props. Majority to Russia or Burma in 1943. Small batch retained by Royal Navy as Sea Hurricane Mk XIIA.

Sea Hurricane Mk IA. Camship catapult launched variant for one way operation. Total of 50 conversions from Mk I

Sea Hurricane Mk IB. Fully navalised variant with catapult spools and arrester A frame hook. 340 converted from Mk IIA Series 2.

Sea Hurricane Mk IC. Standard IB variant with four cannon wing. 400 conversions from IIB and IIC land fighters.

Sea Hurricane Mk IIC. Mk IIC land version fully navalised. 400 conversions from IIC land fighters.

A rocket firing Hurricane IV fitted with additional armour protection.

Hurricane KX405, Mk IV, during trials. It was converted at a later stage to Mk IV standards.

Mk IV(Trop), No. 6 Squadron, Totoi, Greece, late 1944. LF 498. Empty rails suggest aircraft in landing mode.

Mk IVs, No. 531 Yugoslav Squadron, Prkos Island, 1944.

Mk IV, No. 351 Yugoslav Squadron, Prkos Island, 1944.

Mk IV over Irrawaddy River, Aya Bridge, near Mandalay, 1945.

Mk IV with typical load. Eight 3in rockets and long range tanks. Balkan airfield.

Mk IV presentation machine by Fiji.

A line-up of the Irish Air Corps' Hurricane Is and IIs at Baldonnel 1945.

LF363, the last surviving RAF Hurricane in full flying trim, though without its wartime camouflage.

In 1948 Z3687, an early Hurricane II, was used by the RAE Farnborough for wing-flow tests.

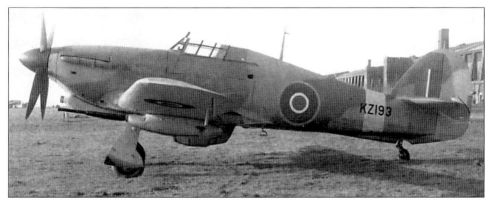

The first Hurricane V prototype, KZ193, with a ground-boosted Merlin 32 engine and a 4-blade Rotol propeller.

CHAPTER TEN

Camouflage and Markings

By the end of 1936 the camouflage patterns for Hawker's F.36/34 High Speed Interceptor, named Hurricane in the June of that year, had been developed at the Royal Aircraft Establishment, Farnborough (RAE). Up to this period only the upper surfaces of day fighters were camouflaged, the under surfaces being finished in the standard aluminium (silver) dope scheme. The colours, dark green and dark earth were specified to be used on fighter monoplanes (unlike biplanes which were to use the additional colours light earth and light green). A camouflage pattern diagram for the Hurricane was drawn up by the Royal Aircraft Establishment (RAE) to provide a guide of the areas to be covered by the two colours, and this was subsequently translated into a large camouflage and markings drawing by Hawker Aircraft for the use of production lines, repair units and the Services.

The basic Hurricane pattern remained unchanged on production aircraft throughout the life of the aeroplane, albeit with colour changes to suit operational requirements and roles. The original diagram for the Hurricane specified red and blue roundels on upper wing surfaces and fuselage sides, but it was considered that the collision risk in peacetime necessitated the adoption of more conspicuous markings.

The peacetime roundel evolved by the RAE consisted of rings of matt red, white and matt blue, all surrounded by an outer ring of yellow with all rings being of equal width, i.e. the red centre was 1/7th, white 3/7ths and blue 5/7ths. This style of roundel was known as the type A1, and on the upper wing surfaces of the Hurricane a diameter of 49ins (seven ring widths of 7in) was specified. Those on the fuselage were 35in diameter (seven ring widths of 5in). The under wing roundels were dull red, white and dull blue of 45in diameter (five ring widths of 9in). Serial letters and numbers, painted in black under the wings, were 30in high and positioned inboard of the roundel. Under war conditions, when greater risks were acceptable, it was intended the red and blue roundel be re-instated.

Hurricane Mark Is first entered service with the Royal Air Force at Northolt, Middlesex, with No. 111 Squadron in December 1937. They were painted in peacetime camouflage as described. After the squadron was fully equipped the fins were adorned with the Unit's crest, and some time later with the squadron number in a position aft of the fuselage roundel. Squadron Leader Gillian's Hurricane had this number painted in white, but other aeroplanes had the upper part of the number in the Flight colours, the lower half in white. This was the system originally tested by No. 3 Squadron and later by other units.

At the period of introduction of camouflage to fighters it was considered necessary only to apply a matt finish to upper surfaces in order to render them less conspicuous when viewed from the air, either in flight over varying terrain or parked

In early 1937 Air Marshal Sir Hugh Dowding, C-in-C, Fighter Command, had suggested a system of providing instant recognition of defending fighters by having the underside of the port wing painted black. Initially it was thought the remainder of the under surface be left in its original aluminium finish, but this was dismissed in favour of an even more distinctive marking with the port wing black and the starboard white. The scheme was tested on a number of obsolete biplanes, such as the Gauntlet, and declared to be effective, but one officer complained that while the white was distinctive at height, black was inconspicuous, making the aeroplane more difficult to recognise.

Service trials with the first fifty Hurricanes were decided upon, but as they were too advanced on the production lines, or in service, the decision was changed to introduce the scheme on Hurricanes L1576 to L1625. Prior to this there had been some discussion about under wing serials on the black and white surfaces. The protagonists for keeping the numbers insisted they provided some identification if the aeroplane was sighted flying low and the pilot could be reprimanded. The consensus of opinion was to keep the letters and numerals.

The new scheme agreed for the Hurricane was port wing from tip to centre section (up to the joint fairing) to be painted black with white serial, and the starboard white with black serial. Roundels in the existing size would be situated in their normal positions. The fuselage section between the wings, and what remained of the under surfaces were to be left in normal aluminium. This was to produce a three-colour scheme.

Mk II(T) reveals the black (night) and white (or aluminium) under surfaces. The wing roundel on the black wing had a yellow outer ring.

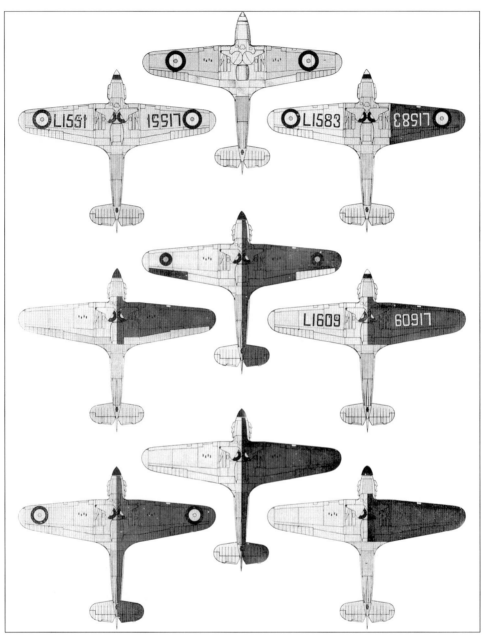

Under surface colours for early Hurricanes varied quite considerably. The schemes illustrated above were in use from 1939 to June 1940. Full details of the colour schemes and roundel sizes are given in Chapter Ten.

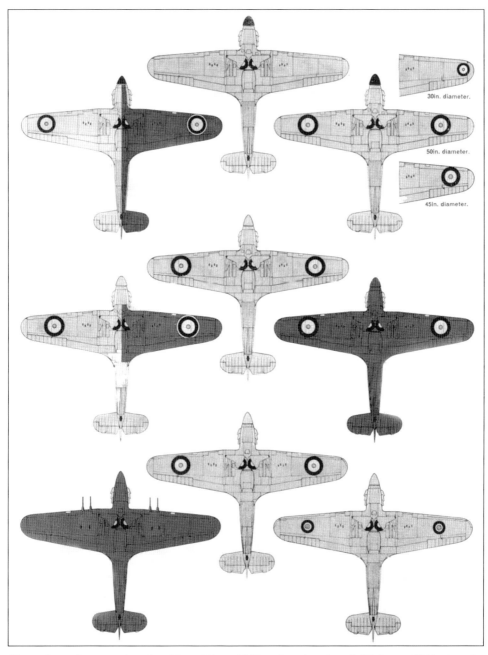

30in. diameter.

50in. diameter.

45in. diameter.

Sky under surfaces were introduced from 6 June 1940 and continued until 15 August 1941 when sky was replaced by medium sea grey. A short re-introduction of the black port wing was made in November 1940 but soon disappeared. The night fighter finish, 'special night', was introduced on 22 May 1940 to be replaced with 'smooth night' finish on 19 October 1942. (See Chapter Ten)

After a number of Hurricanes adorned with the new scheme had been flown by members of several squadrons for assessment, it was suggested that aircraft of the test batch not yet painted should have the black and white areas of the wings extended to the centre line of the fuselage. The fifty machines were completed and delivered, but the Air Ministry decided to reintroduce the all aluminium under surface for future production aircraft. Fighter Command hierarchy, however, was convinced of the value of the black and white scheme as a quick aid to recognition, and it was to be adopted later as standard and reintroduced on the Hurricane production lines.

During the Munich crisis of late summer 1938, the standard war markings were specified and the brighter, peacetime schemes replaced by dull tints on all operational fighters, bombers and Army co-operation aeroplanes. The peacetime roundels of Hurricanes were converted by retaining the dull blue ring, enlarging the red centre to 2/5ths of the blue diameter and extending the blue inwards to the red centre, over painting the inner white ring. The yellow outer ring was also over painted, being covered by the camouflage tones of dark green or earth to match the overall pattern. The converted roundels were 35in in diameter on the upper wing and 25in on fuselage sides.

At this time of the national emergency the under surface scheme displayed a variety of styles, with some aeroplanes in the original black and white, or aluminium – as tried on the fifty test Hurricanes, plus a number with only the port wing under surface in black, or night, and the remaining surface in aluminium. Other aircraft had the port and starboard wing in night and white respectively with the under fuselage, including centre section, and tailplane in aluminium. These schemes were obviously the result of confused instructions, or oversight, and in a number of instances Hurricanes were sighted with the serial numbers displayed on the under surfaces.

When the aeroplanes were painted at their home base the ailerons were, normally, left in their original silver finish, but on a number the control surfaces of the wings were painted in night or white and they were liable to become over balanced due to the weight of the paint. It was normal for the under wing roundels to be deleted or painted over, but

Mk IIA, Z4769 had light green patches on rear fuselage and tail, remainder black. En route to Egypt with long range underwing tanks.

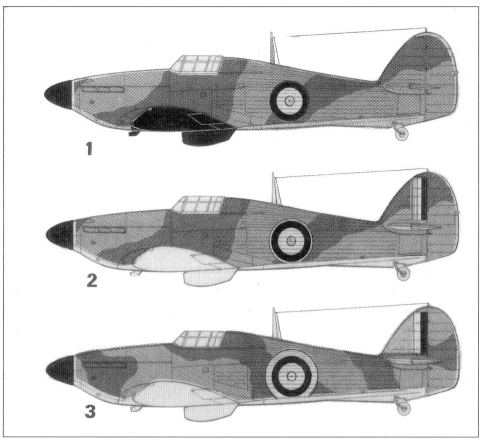

(1) Standard production schemes for hurricanes during early 1940. Dark green, dark earth uppers with night, white and aluminium under surfaces. Type A roundels.

(2) Conversion of above scheme with narrow fin stripes and a narrow outer yellow roundel ring to fuselage roundel. Conformed to Signal X.485. Under surfaces either night, white and aluminium or (after 6 June 1940) sky or home-mixed equivalent.

(3) Another conversion of the early 1940 colour scheme. Broader outer yellow roundel ring (same width as dark blue ring). Entire fin painted with dull red forward section and fairly narrow white and dull blue stripes. Development of this fin scheme eventually adopted as a standard but with wider (nine inch) white and dull blue stripes.

Upper and under surfaces of Hurricanes.

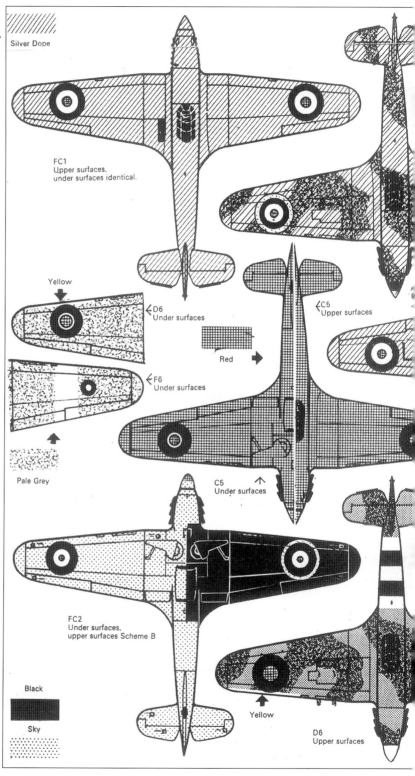

Silver Dope

FC1
Upper surfaces,
under surfaces identical.

Yellow

←D6
Under surfaces

←C5
Upper surfaces

Red

←F6
Under surfaces

Pale Grey

C5
Under surfaces

FC2
Under surfaces,
upper surfaces Scheme B

Black

Sky

Yellow

D6
Upper surfaces

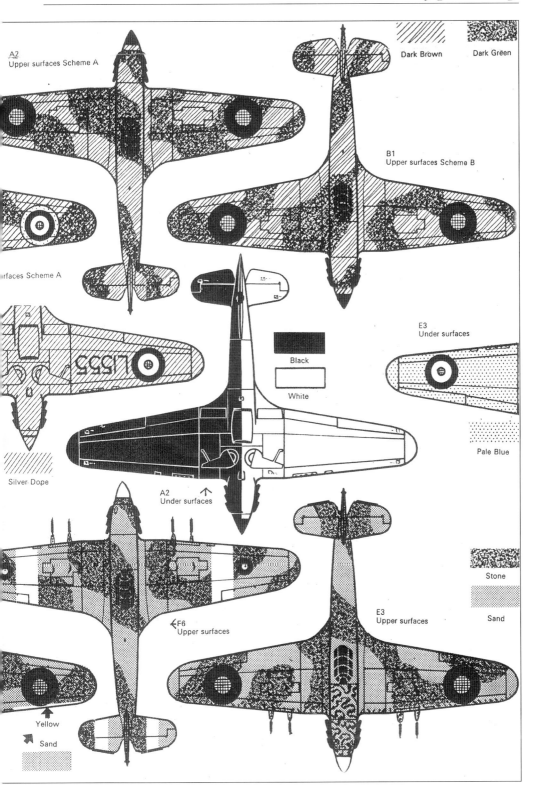

A2
Upper surfaces Scheme A

B1
Upper surfaces Scheme B

Dark Brown

Dark Green

...rfaces Scheme A

Black

White

E3
Under surfaces

Pale Blue

Silver Dope

A2
Under surfaces

F6
Upper surfaces

E3
Upper surfaces

Stone

Sand

Yellow

Sand

Mk II(Trop), BM565. Matt black and white under surfaces. Relegated to unarmed trainer. Flew in India with GATO until 1947.

in a number of instances they were converted to red and blue only.

The many variations in Service painting of the night and white scheme were, to some extent, the result of ambiguous directives. For instance, a number of Hurricanes had the entire surfaces painted night and white in equal proportions, night to port and white to starboard and the scheme included the under fuselage from nose to tail and tailplane. In an attempt to clarify the situation a directive was issued which stated only the rear of the fuselage between the leading and trailing edge of the wings need be painted in the two colours. This resulted in the Hurricane having a half wing to the centre line in either night or white with the nose portion and aft fuselage in silver, this to include the tailplane.

A major change in markings due to the emergency regulations of 1938 was the Squadron identification numbers being replaced by two letters positioned on one side of the fuselage roundel, with the individual aircraft letter on the opposite side. These 'Code letters' were painted in a special colour evolved at RAE for the purpose, and was known initially as 'grey', the official Service parlance calling it 'lettering, grey'. But the technical term was sea grey, DTD 33B/157. It was also called medium sea grey, or sea grey medium. The latter title was often quoted on official camouflage diagrams and documents, although the colour was always intended to be medium sea grey as was confirmed later in the war.

By the late spring of 1939 the majority of operational Hurricanes had been converted to wartime markings, but a number could still be seen in the original, peacetime delivery scheme, or even in a semi-converted state. Most of these were normally reserve aircraft at the MUs. By the outbreak of war in September most of the squadrons and training units (OTUs) were flying fighters in the approved, standard scheme of dark earth and dull red type B roundels on upper surfaces, but the under surfaces still had variations of black and white, with the majority having the colours painted from wing tip to aircraft centre line, plus the silver fuselage and tailplane. Medium sea grey code and aircraft letters were positioned on either side of the fuselage roundel.

Roundels were not normally painted on the wing under surface at this time with one exception, the Hurricanes that were despatched to France as part of the Air Component of the British Expeditionary Force (BEF). Two Hurricane squadrons, Nos 1 and 73, formed No. 67 Wing of the Advanced Striking Force, and these units flew their Hurricanes with their rudders painted in dull red, white and blue stripes, possibly to match the style of the locally based French fighters. In general the French-based Hurricanes had one MSG letter aft of the fuselage roundel, although a few did carry the squadron code letters in addition.

During the late autumn of 1939 a serious recognition error brought about a change of markings in an effort to make British aircraft more easily identifiable. A telegram, A949/32, was sent to all Commands on 30 October ordering that type B roundels on upper wing surfaces had to be changed to type A – red, white and blue. Other telegrams ordered all aeroplanes, with the exception of fighters and night bombers, to have type A roundels under wing tips. The wording of the telegrams was, to say the least, ambiguous and there was confusion over interpretation. Consequently, on 21 November all Commands were again notified that only general reconnaissance maritime aircraft, Sunderlands, Lerwicks, Ansons would carry the type A roundel on upper wings, but all aircraft would have them in place of the type B on fuselage sides. On Hurricanes the type A roundels, when converted from the type B, were either 25 or 35in diameter, but new production aeroplanes had 35in.

From combat experience it was decided that RAF national markings were still inconspicuous, and as a result on 1 May 1940 Signal X485 was despatched to all Commands. This ordered the yellow outer roundel ring of pre-war days was to be re-instated to the fuselage roundels, and that red, white and blue stripes be added to each side of the fin. Once again the signal was subject to interpretation and a wide variety of fin stripes appeared, this despite a number of additional signals.

The outer yellow ring was specified as being the same width as the blue, but where space was limited, such as the Spitfire fuselage, a narrow yellow ring would be acceptable. On the Hurricane the type A ring was 25in in diameter and it converted the type A1 of 35in. Where the ring was 35in it converted into a 49in A1. However, there were a number of instances where the 35in A was outlined with a narrow yellow ring.

Fin stripes varied, in some instances 5, 6 or 7in widths of red, white and blue were used. In

Familiar photograph of L1592 when with No. 56 Squadron North Weald and No. 45 at Tabgemere during the Battle of Britain. Note the large grey codes and four colour fuselage rings.

137

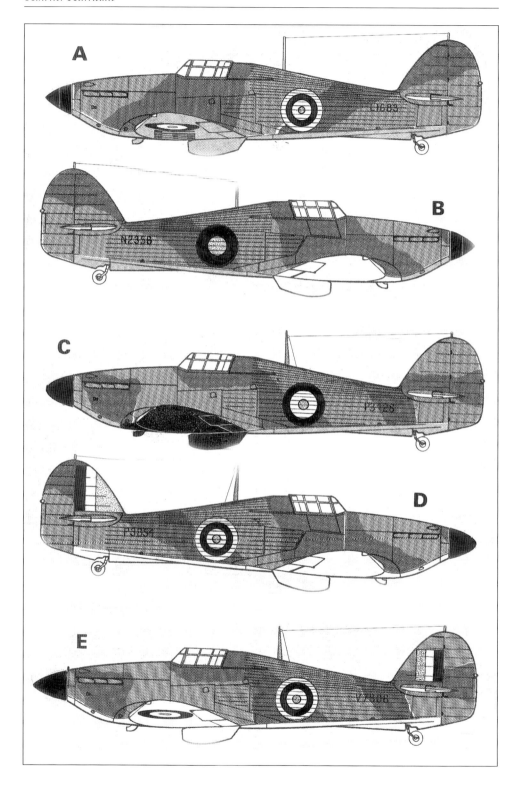

Hurricane Mk IIC with four cannon ring. Upper surfaces scheme shows the irregular scheme of dark earth and dark green. Yellow stripe along outer wing sections leading edges. Note also sky ring around rear fuselage.

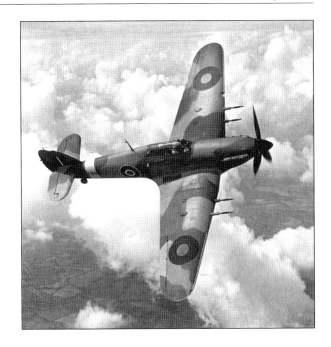

others the entire forward section of the fin was painted red, followed by the other two colours. The standard style was 9in wide stripes of blue and white with the front of the fin in red.

On 15 May 1940 Signal X296 ordered that all under wing roundels of red, white and blue be applied to all fighter aircraft. This was followed by a second message, X479, which stated all the roundel on the black wing was to be outlined in yellow of type A convenient width. On 6 June Signal X915 brought about another major change in fighter markings for it laid down that the black and white under surfaces to be replaced by an overall sky finish to match the 'colour of an average sky over the British Isles at medium altitudes' – about 10,000 feet.

Sky was in too short supply at the depots to make a general issue possible, and the Air Ministry confused that situation once again by sending out instructions to the effect that, 'Until sky became readily available, the original black and white scheme would continue to be used'. It was all very confusing, more so when supplies of the official sky mixture was insufficient to cope with demand, and a number of service units mixed their own.

Opposite: *Development of standard roundels, fin stripes and under surface schemes.*
(A) L1683 lacks fin stripes, has broad outer yellow roundel fuselage ring and standard under wing roundels. Aluminium unders.
(B) N2358 with broad dull blue outer and white inner ringed roundel. No fin stripes. Night and white (or aluminium) unders.
(C) P3428 had standard three ring coloured roundel, large black spinner and night and white unders.
(D) P3854 had the same overall scheme as (A) but entire fin with forward red followed by white and dull blue stripes.
(E) V7806 had same scheme as (A) and (D) but panel of red, white and blue stripes on fin.

Some with a basic blue tint and others with green. As the colour came into general use a new version, type S with a smoother finish was issued in place of type M. As a result all aeroplane paints in the smooth finish had the suffix S applied.

With the appearance of the single tone under surface roundels also disappeared. At a meeting of the Air Staff on 23 July 1940 a decision was taken to re-instate under surface roundels and the order passed down the line on 11 August. Hurricanes had 50in roundels and a standardised 27 by 24in high fin flash of three equal widths of 8in. With the end of the Battle of Britain in October 1940, a review of camouflage schemes for fighters was once again undertaken and it was planned to reintroduce the old black and white under wing markings. In the event only the black was used with the starboard wing painted sky. The black was a semi-permanent, washable distemper and roundels were applied. The port had a yellow outer ring. This scheme lasted until April 1941. A sky painted spinner was introduced on 27 November in addition to an 18in wide sky band around the rear fuselage.

A large number of Hurricane Mk Is were being sent overseas to the Middle East. They were painted in the normal temperate scheme of dark green and earth with azure blue under surfaces. Spinners were often painted red. By mid-1941 a new colour scheme was being introduced to home-based fighters with the earth areas over painted in dark sea grey, a mix of medium sea grey and night. An alternative colour was ocean grey. This scheme was changed to a pattern of sand earth with blue unders.

APPENDIX I

Hurricane Production Contracts

Contract No. 357483/34. F36/34 prototype K5083. Powered by Rolls-Royce Merlin C. First flown at Brooklands, 6 November 1935.

First Hawker production batch. 600 aeroplanes. L1547-L2146. Aircraft delivered overseas. Poland L2048. South Africa L1708, L1710, L1711. Yugoslavia (12) L1751, L1752, L1837-L1840, L1858-L1863. Romania (12) L2077, L2078, L2085, L2093-L2097, L2104, L2112-L2114. Canada (22) L1759-L1763, L1878-L1890, L2021-L2023, L2144. L1848 delivered as pattern aircraft. Belgium (20) L1918-L1920, L1993-L1997, L2040-L2044, L2105-L2111. Persia L2079. Turkey (15) L2125-L2139.

Second Hawker production batch. 300 aeroplanes. N2318-N2367, N2380-N2409, N2422-N2441, N2453-N2502, N2520-N2559, N2582-N2631, N2645-N2729. Aircraft shipped to Poland but diverted to Middle East, September 1939 N2322-N2324, N2327, N2349, N2392-N2935. Yugoslavia (12) N2718-N2729.

First Gloster production batch. 500 aeroplanes. First flight 20 October 1939. P2535-P2584, P2614-P2653, P2672-P2701, P2713-P2732, P2751-P2770, P2792-P2836, P2854-P2888, P2900-P2924, P2946-P2995, P3020-P3069, P3080- P3124, P3140-P3179, P3200-P3234, P3250-P3264.

Second Gloster production batch. 100 aeroplanes. R4074-R4123, R4171-R4200, R4213-R4232.

Third Gloster production batch. Part 1. 500 aeroplanes. V6533-V6582, V6600-V6649, V6665-V6704, V6722-V6761, V6776-V6825, V6840-V6889, V6913-V6932, V6969-V6952, V6979-V7028, V7042-V7081, V7099-V7138, V7156-V7195. Part 2. 200 aeroplanes. W9110-W9159, W9170-W9209, W9215-W9244, W9260-W9279, W9290-W9329, W9340-W9359. Part 3. 519 aeroplanes. Z4022-Z4071, Z4085-Z4119, Z4161-Z4205, Z4223-Z4292, Z4308-Z4327, Z4347-Z4391, Z4415-Z4434, Z4482-Z4516, Z4532-Z4581, Z4603-Z4652, Z4686-Z4720, Z4760-Z4809, Z4832-Z4865.

Third Hawker production batch. 530 aeroplanes. P3265-P3279, P3300-P3324, P3345-P3364, P3380-P3429, P3448-P3492, P3515-P3554, P3574-P3623, P3640-P3684, P3700-P3739, P3755-P3789, P3802-P3836, P3854-P3903, P3920-P3944, P3960-P3984, P8809-P8818, R2680-R2689, T9519-T9538, W6667-W6670.

Fourth Hawker production batch. 500 aeroplanes. V7200-V7209, V7221-V7260, V7276-V7318, V7337-V7396, V7400-V7446, V7461-V7510, V7533-V7572, V7588-V7627, V7644-V7690, V7705-V7737, V7741-V7780, V7795-V7838, V7851-V7862, AS987-AS990.

Canadian production batch. Canadian Car & Foundry Corporation. 40 aeroplanes. P5170-P5209.

Appendix II

Production Batches

The following details of production Hurricanes are based upon material currently available. The serial number is followed by the Mark number; specific details and destination if serving abroad. A large number of Hurricanes were subjected to a re-manufacturing process which altered the basic production specification. Where this occurred a new serial number was applied.

K5083. Hawker F.36/34 Hurricane prototype ordered under Contract No. 357483/34 and dated 18 February 1935. Powered by a Rolls-Royce Merlin II engine. One 2-blade, fixed pitch propeller. First flight 6 November 1935 from Brooklands, Surrey. Pilot P.W.S. Bulman. Subjected to numerous trials including handling; engine and undercarriage tests; handling at various weightings; aileron tests; diving; fuel pressure; armament installed; hood tests; take off; spins; new radiator; R/T; aerobatics.

Hawker Hurricane 15/36, Mk I, (Hawker). First Contract, No. 527112/36, dated 3 June 1936. Serial numbers L1547 to L2146. Initial production run delivered between 15 December 1937 to 6 October 1939. Initial production a/c powered by Merlin II and Watts 2-blade, fixed pitch wood propeller. Later deliveries had Merlin III with Rotol or DH VP/CS. Basic wing structure fabric covered. Many modified at later date.

L1547, 1st prod. F/F 12.10.37. Trials at Brooklands, Rolls-Royce, Hucknall and Martlesham Heath. Handling; undercarriage; performance; climb and level speed; propeller; stability; oil cooling; spins.
L1562. Martlesham Heath. Conv to Mk IIA, metal wings. Shipped Russia as DR344.
L1574. Martlesham Heath.
L1582. Tests of camouflage schemes.
L1589. To Boulton Paul for comparison tests with Defiant.
L1596. Martlesham Heath for night flying trials. Conv to Mk IIA metal wings as DG618.
L1606. Trials with Rotol propellers. Seconded to Hawkers as G-AFKX.
L1607. Comparative tests with Defiant.
L1638. Trials hydraulic systems.
L1669. To Rolls-Royce, Hucknall, engine trials. Tropical trials in M.E. as Mk I(T).
L1684. Conv to Mk IIA as DR354. Shipped Russia.
L1695. Martlesham Heath for Rotol and DH propeller trials.
L1696. Martlesham Heath for slotted wing trials.
L1702. Farnborough, handling trials. To Boscombe Down.
L1708, L1710, L1711. Shipped South Africa, SAAF.
L1713. Merlin II trials, Rolls-Royce, Hucknall. To Farnborough with L1717 for same.
L1717. Farnborough, balloon cable cutting trials. See also above.
L1750. Martlesham Heath. Additional cockpit armour and 2x20mm Oerlikon cannon under wings. Trials during BoB.
L1751, L1752. Shipped to Yugoslavia.
L1759(310), 1760(311), 1761(312), 1762(313),

1763(314). To RCAF, Canada, October 1938. New RCAF serials in brackets.
L1769. Conv to Mk IIA as DR359. Shipped Russia.
L1831. Conv to Mk IIA as DR642.
L1837(3-291), 1838(4-292), 1839(5-293), 1840(6-294). Shipped to Yugoslavia. L1843, L1844. Metal wings conv.
L1848. To Canada as pattern a/c 2.3.39.
L1855. Metal wings conv.
L1856. T.I of Merlin XII, R-R. Mods back to Mk I.
L1877. T.I of metal wings. Used for tropical air filter trials.
L1858(7-312), 1859(8-313), 1860(9-314), 1861(10-315), 1862(11-316), 1863(12- 317). Shipped to Yugoslavia.
L1878(315), 1879(316), 1881(318), 1882(319), 1883(320), 1884(321), 1885(322), 1886(323), 1887(324), 1890(326).
L1884 used for trials with Hillson slip wing in 1943.
L1898. Con to Sea Hurricane Mk IA.
L1899, 1903, 1904, 1905, 1906, 1907, 1917. Metal wings convs.
L1918, 1919, 1920. Shipped to Belgium.
L1962, 1963, 1964, 1965, 1966, 1967, 1968, 1969, 1970, 1971, 1972, 1973, 1974, 1975, 1976, 1977, 1978, 1979, 1980, 1981, 1982, 1983, 1984, 1985, 1986, 1987, 1988, 1989, 1990, 1991, 1992. Metal wings convs.
L1993, 1994, 1995, 1996, 1997. Shipped to Belgium.
L1998, 1999, 2000, 2002, 2003, 2004, 2005. Metal wings convs.
L2021, 2022, 2023. To RCAF.
L2024, 2025. Shipped to Turkey.

L2026. Martlesham Heath.
L2027, 2028, 2029, 2030, 2031, 2032, 2033.
Shipped to Turkey.
L2040, 2041, 2042, 2043, 2044. Shipped to
Belgium.
L2048. Shipped to Poland.
L2077, 2078. Shipped to Romania.
L2079. Shipped to Persia.
L2085. Shipped to Romania.
L2086. Conv to Sea Hurricane 1A.
L2093, 2094, 2095, 2096, 2097. Shipped to

Romania.
L2099. Conv to Mk IIA.
2104. Shipped to Romania.
L2105, 2106, 2107, 2108, 2109, 2110, 2111.
Shipped to Belgium.
L2112, 2113, 2114, 2125, 2126, 2127, 2128, 2129,
2130, 2131, 2132, 2133, 2134, 2135, 2136, 2137,
2138, 2139. Shipped to Turkey.
L2144. To Canada a pattern a/c.

Hurricane Mk I. 300 aircraft produced under Contract No. 751458/38 dated 3 September 1940. First 80 models with fabric covered wings; remainder metal. Merlin II with Rotol or DH CS/CP propellers. Delivered between 29 September 1940 to 1 May 1940. Serial numbers. N2318-2367, 2380-2409, 2422-2441, 2453-2502, 2520-2559, 2582-2631, 2645-2729.

N2318. To R-R for engine mods and trials.
N2322, 2323, 2324, 2327. Shipped to Poland.
N2346. Boscombe Down for performance trials.
N2350. Scheduled as first two-seat trainer.
Cancelled.
N2351, 2352, 2367. Conv to Sea Hurricane IA.
N2392, 2393, 2394, 2395. Original sale to Poland.
Contract cancelled on outbreak of war.
N2409. Conv to Sea Hurricane Mk IA.
N2422. First production a/c with metal wings
N2429, 2433. Production metal wings.
N2466. Hydraulic systems trials Hawkers.
N2467, 2468, 2469. Conv to Sea Hurricane Mk
IA.
L2479. Conv to Mk IIA as BV168.
L2488, 2489. Conv to Sea Hurricane Mk IA.

L2498, 2499. Mk I(T).
N2541. Used for de-icing trials.
N2544. Conv to Mk IIA by R-R as DG616.
N2590, 2591, 2599. Conv to Sea Hurricane Mk
IA.
N2602. Conv to Mk IIA as BV172.
N2607. Conv to Mk IIA by R-R as DG633.
N2618. Conv to Sea Hurricane Mk IA.
N2624, 2625, 2626, 2628. Mk I(T).
N2630, 2631. Conv to Sea Hurricane Mk IA.
N2646. Hydraulics trials, Hawkers. N2648, 2660.
Conv to Sea Hurricane Mk IA.
N2666. Conv to Mk IIA as DR367. To Russia.
N2718, 2719, 2720, 2721, 2722, 2723, 2724, 2725,
2726m, 2727, 2728, 2729. Shipped to Yugoslavia.

Hurricane Mk I (Gloster). 500 aircraft produced under Contract No. 962371/38/C.23A. Merlin III with DHVP or Rotol CS propellers. First flight 20 November 1939. Delivery between November 1939 to April 1940. Serial numbers 2535-2584, 2614-2653, 2672-2701, 2713-2732, 2751-2770, 2792-2836, 2854-2888, 2900-2924, 2946-2995, 3030-3069, 3080-3124, 3140-3179, 3200-3234, 3250-3264.

P2544. Mk I(T).
P2627. Mk I(T). Mods to PR(T)I.
P2639, 2640, 2641, 2643, 2651. Mk I(T).
P2682. Conv to Mk IIA as DG641 by R-R.
P2731. Conv to Sea Hurricane Mk IA.
P2823. Conv to Mk IIA as BV161.
P2829(DR355), 2835(DR353), 2904(DR357),
2908(DR369). To Russia.
P2863. Con to Mk IIA.
P2925. Con to Mk IIA.
P2940, 2953, 2963. Conv to Sea Hurricane Mk
IA.
P2968. To Eire 107.
P2972. Conv to Sea Hurricane Mk IA.
P2975. Conv to Mk IIA as DR372. To Russia.
P2986. Conv to Sea Hurricane IA.
P2989. Trials Boscombe Down with 2x250lb wing
bombs.
P2992, 3020 Conv to Sea Hurricane Mk IA.
P3023. Conv to Mk IIA as BV169.

P3036, 3056. Conv to Sea Hurricane Mk IA.
P3057. Conv to Mk IIA as DG615 by R-R.
P3067. Mk I(T).
P3068. Conv to Mk IIA as DG615 by R-R.
P3090, 3092. Conv to Sea Hurricane IA.
P3103. Conv to Mk IIA as DR340.
P3104. Conv to Sea Hurricane Mk IA.
P3106. Conv to Mk IIA as DR370. To Russia.
P3111. Conv to Sea Hurr Mk IA.
P3114. Conv to Sea Hurricane Mk I.
P3121. Conv to Mk IIA as DR350. To Russia.
P3151. Conv to Mk IIA.
P3152. Conv to Sea Hurricane Mk IA.
P3157. T.I. Performance trials, Boscombe Down.
P3165, 3168, 3206. Conv to Sea Hurricane Mk
IA.
P3207. Conv to Mk IIA(DG631),3223(DG614)
by R-R.
PP3229. Conv to Sea Hurricane Mk IA.
P3256. Conv to Mk IIA as DR365. To Russia.

Hurricane Mk I (Hawker). 500 aircraft produced under Contract No. 962371/38. Merlin III, metal wings. Delivered between 21 February 1940 and 20 July 1940. Merlin III. Serials. P3265-3279, 3300-3324, 3345-3364, 3380-3429, 3448-3492, 3515-3554, 3574-3623, 3640-3684, 3700-3739, 3755-3789, 3802-3836, 3854-3903, 3920-3944, 3960-3984. Plus batch of 44 replacement aircraft. P8809-8818, R2680-2689, T9519-9538, W6667-6670.

P3265. Prototype Hurricane Mk II. Merlin XX. Trials of rear view hood. Became maintenance airframe October 1942.
P3270. Conv to Mk I(T).
P3301. Conv to Sea Hurricane Mk IA.
P3309. Conv to Mk IIA as DR364. To Russia.
P3345. Trials with various camouflage schemes.
P3351. Conv to Mk IIA as DR393. To Russia.
P3362, 3394. Conv to Sea Hurricane Mk IA.
P3412. Conv to Mk IIA as DG613.
P3416. To Eire 108.
P3449. Conv to Mk IIA as DR362. To Russia.
P3460. Conv to Sea Hurricane Mk IA.
P3462. Trials with overload fuel tanks.
P3466, 3467. Conv to Sea Hurricane Mk IA.
P3521. Conv to Mk IIA as BV167.
P3525. To Boscombe Down.
P3530. Conv to Sea Hurricane Mk IA.
P3539. Conv to Mk IIA as DG634 by R-R.
P3544. Conv to Sea Hurricane Mk IA.
P3551. Conv to Mk IIA as DR343. To Russia.
P3597. Conv to Sea Hurricane Mk IA.
P3620. Conv to Sea Hurrivane Mk IA by Gen A/Ct.
P3641. Radio trials at TRE Malvern.
P3670. Conv to Mk IIA as DG646 by R-R.
P3705. Conv to Mk I(T).
P3706. Conv to Sea Hurricane Mk IA.
P3710. Conv to Sea Hurricane Mk IA by Gen A/Ct.
P3714(DR341), 3717(DR348). Conv to Mk IIA. To Russia.

P3719. Conv to Sea Hurricane Mk IA by Gen A/Ct.
P3720. Shipped to Persia.
P3722, 3723, 3724, 3729, 3731, 3732, 3733, 3734. Conv to Mk I(T).
P3736. Fuel consumption trials.
P3756(DG612), 3759(DG349 Russia). Conv to Mk IIA.
P3773, 3776, 3784, 3805. Conv to Sea Hurricane Mk IA by Gen A/Ct.
P3811. Twelve gun wings. Propeller trials. Conv to Mk IIA as DG644.
P3814. Con to Sea Hurricane Mk IA by Gen A/Ct.
P3818. Conv to Mk I(T).
P3820. Engine and performance trials.
P3821, 3822. Conv to Mk I(T).
P3823. Engine and performance trials.
P3828. Conv to Mk IIA as DR363. To Russia.
P3829. Conv to Sea Hurricane Mk IA.
P3830. Trials of rear view hood.
P3870, 3877, 3883. Conv to Sea Hurricane Mk IA by Gen A/Ct.
P3923. Performance trials with Rotol propellers.
P3924, 3925, 3926. Conv to Sea Hurricane Mk IA.
P3928. Conv to Mk IIA as DR363. To Russia.
P3934. Conv to Sea Hurricane Mk IA.
P3967, 3969, 3970. Conv to Mk I(T).
P3975, 3979. Conv to Sea Hurricane Mk IA.
T9523. Conv to Mk I(T).

Hurricane Mk I (Canada). 40 aircraft. Merlin II and III. Serials. P5170-5209.

P5170. Trials at Farnborough and Boscombe Down March 1940.
P5176. Forced landing, Eire. To 93.

P5183. Conv to Sea Hurricane Mk IA by Gen A/Ct.

Hurricane Mk I (Gloster). 100 aircraft produced under Contract No. 19773/39/2A. Merlin II with DH or Rotol propellers. Delivered between May to July 1940. Serials. R4074-4123, 4171-4200, 4213-4132.

R4077, 4078. Conv to Sea Hurricane Mk IA by Gen A/Ct.
R4081. Conv to Mk IIA as DR358. To Russia.
R4088. Conv to Sea Hurricane Mk IA.
R4091. Conv to Mk IIA as DR373.
R4095. Conv to Sea Hurricane Mk IA.

R4103, 4104. To SAAF.
R4105, 4177, 4178, 4214. Conv to Sea Hurricane Mk IA by Gen A/Ct.
R4218. Conv to Mk IIA(T) as BV155.
R4226. Conv to Sea Hurricane Mk IA.

Hurricane Mk I (Gloster) 1,700 aircraft produced under Contract No. 85730/40/C.23a. Merlin III with DH or Rotol propellers. First Order 500 a/c. Delivered July to November 1940. Serials. V6533-6582, 6600-6049, 6665-6704, 6722-6761, 6776-6825, 6840-6889, 6913-6962, 6979-7028, 7042-7081, 7099-7138,7156-7195.

V6535. Conv to Mk IIA Srs I as DG630 by R-R.
V6536, 6537. Conv to Sea Hurricane Mk IA by Gen A/Ct.V6538. Conv to Mk IIA Srs I as DR374. To Russia
V6545. Conv to Sea Hurricane Mk IA.
V6546. Conv to Mk IIA Srs I as DR374. To Russia.
V6552. Conv to Mk I Trainer.
V6555, 6556. Conv to Sea Hurricane Mk IA.
V6557. Radio trials at TRE Malvern.
V6564. Conv to Sea Hurricane IA.
V6576. To Eire 111.
V6577. Conv to Sea Hurricane Mk IA.
V6582(DR639), 6602(DR638). Conv to Mk IIA Srs I.
V6610. Conv to Sea Hurricane Mk IA by Gen A/Ct.
V6613. To Eire 107.
V6649, 6697, 6700, 6723, 6731. Conv to Sea Hurricane Mk IA. by Gen A/Ct.
V6735. Conv to Mk IIA, Srs I.
V6738. Conv to PR Mk I(T).
V6739. Conv to Mk IIA as DR352. To Russia.
V6741. Conv to Sea Hurricane Mk IC.
V6747. Conv to Mk I(T).
V6751, 6756. Conv to Sea Hurricane Mk IA.
V6757. Conv to Mk IIA, Srs I as DG619 by R-R.
V6759, 6760, 6779. Conv to Sea Hurricane Mk IA.
V6785(BV158), 6790(BV156). Conv to Mk IIA, Srs I.
V6794, 6799, 6802, 6815, 6817, 6843. Conv to Sea Hurricane Mk IA by Gen A/Ct.
V6853. Conv to Mk IIA, Srs I as DG643 by R-R.
V6858. Conv to Sea Hurricane Mk IA.
V6861. Conv to Mk IIA, Srs I as DG650 by R-R.
V6867, 6881, 6886. Conv to Sea Hurricane Mk

IA by Gen A/Ct.
V6914(BV165), V6915(DR351 Russia). Conv to Mk IIA, Srs I.
V6924. Conv to Sea Hurricane Mk IA.
V6929. Conv to Mk IIA, Srs I as DG647 by R-R.
V6933. Conv to Sea Hurricane Mk IA by Gen A/Ct.
V6934(DG629), 6936(DR360 Russia). Conv to Mk IIA.
V6940. Conv to Mk I(T).
V6942(DR391), 6950(DR624 Russia). Conv to Mk IIA, Srs I.
V6952, 6957. Conv to Sea Hurricane Mk IA.
V6959(DG627), 6999(DG648). Conv to Mk IIA, Srs I by R-R.
V7005. Conv to Sea Hurricane Mk IA.
V7006(DR347), 7018(DR392), 7021((DR294). Conv to Mk IIA. To Russia.
V7027, 7042, 7043, 7046, 7049, 7050. Conv to Sea Hurricane Mk I.
V7054(DR361 Russia), 7061(DR626). Conv to Mk IIA.
V7063. Conv to Sea Hurricane Mk IA.
V7061. Conv to Mk IIA as DR339. To Russia.
V7069. Conv to Mk IIA as DR339.
V7070, 7071, 7077, 7100, 7113, 7129, 7130, 7133, 7135, 7157. Conv to Sea Hurricane Mk IA.
V7158. To Eire 110.
V7161, 7162. Conv to Sea Hurricane Mk IA.
V7168. Conv to Mk I(T).
V7169. Conv to Mk IIA, Srs I.
V7170, 7172. Conv to Sea Hurricane Mk IA.
V7173. To Eire 109.
V7181. Conv to Mk I(T).
V7182, 7189, 7191, 7194, 7195. Conv to Sea Hurricane Mk IA.

Hurricane Mk I (Gloster) Second order for 200 aircraft. Delivered November/December 1940. Serials. W9110-9159, 9170-9209, 9215-9244, 9260-9279, 9290-9329, 9340-9359.

W9115. Conv to Mk I(T). To ME.
W9116. Conv to Mk I(T). To PR I.
B9124, 9128. Conv to Sea Hurricane Mk IA.
W9133, 9141. Conv to Mk I(T). To ME.
W9174. Conv to Sea Hurricane Mk IA.
W9181. Conv to Mk IIA as DG635 by R-R.
W9182, 9188. Conv to Sea Hurricane Mk IA.
W9209, 9215, 9216, 9218, 9219, 9220, 9221, 9222, 9223, 9224. Conv to Sea Hurricane Mk I.
W9225, 9226, 9228, 9231. Conv to Mk I(T). To ME.
W9237. Conv to Sea Hurricane Mk I.
W9238. Conv to Mk I(T). To ME.
W9265. Conv to Mk I(T). To ME. Conv to Mk II as DR356. To Russia.
W9267. Conv to Mk I(T). To ME. To TAC R Mk

I.
W9268, 9269, 9272, 9291. Conv to Mk I(T). To Me.
W9272, 9276, 9277, 9279. Conv to Sea Hurricane Mk I.
W9293, 9299. Conv to Mk I(T). To ME.
W9300. Conv to Mk I(T). To TAC R Mk I.
W9311, 9312, 9313. Conv to Sea Hurricane Mk I.
W9314. Trials with 4x20mm cannon wing (D). Conv to My IIC prototype. To Boscombe Down.
W9315, 9316, 9318, 9319. Conv to Sea Hurricane Mk I.
W9320, 9326, 9328, 9346, 9350, 9352, 9354, 9359. Conv to Mk I(T). To ME.
W9353. Conv to Mk I(T). To PR. Mk I.

Third Order for 400 a/c. Delivered December 1940 to March 1941. Serials. Z4022-4071, 4085-4119, 4161-4205, 4223-4272, 4308-4327, 4347-4391, 4415-4434, 4482-4516, 4532-4581, 4603-4652.

Z4029, 4031, 4036. Conv Mk I(T). To ME.
Z4037. To Eire 106.
Z4039. Conv to Sea Hurricane Mk I.
Z4040, 4047. Conv Mk I(T). To ME.
Z4051, 4053, 4056, 4057. Conv to Sea Hurricane Mk I.
Z4062, 4063, 4064. Conv to Mk I(T). To ME. To TAC R Mk I.
Z4162, 4170, 4172, 4173, 4189, 4190, 4229, 4230, 4231 (Later to PR Mk I), 4233, 4238, 4239, 4252, 4254, 4256, 4257, 4266, 4269, 4272, 4313, 4322, 4338, 4348, 4350, 4361. Conv to Mk I(T). Last five a/c to ME.
Z4365. Conv to Sea Hurricane Mk I.
Z4391. To TAC R Mk I.
Z4419. To Mk I(T). To ME.
Z4483. To Mk I(T). To ME. To TAC R Mk I.
Z4484. Conv to Mk I(T).
Z4489. Conv to Mk II. To ME.
Z4491, 4494. Conv to Mk I(T). To ME.
Z4500, 4504. Conv to Sea Hurricane Mk I.
Z4508. Conv to Mk I(T). To ME
Z4532. Conv to Sea Hurricane Mk I.

Z4544. Conv to Mk I(T). To ME.
Z4550. Conv to Sea Hurricane Mk I.
Z4551. Conv to Mk I(T). To ME.
Z4553. Conv to Sea Hurricane Mk I.
Z4554, 4557, 4561,4563,4564,4566. Conv to Mk I(T). To ME.
Z4568, 4569. Conv to Sea Hurricane Mk I.
Z4574. Conv to Mk I(T). To ME.
Z4576. To Gloster A/Ct as trials aircraft. Mk I(T).
Z4581. Conv to Sea Hurricane Mk I.
Z4604. Conv to Mk I(T). To ME.
Z4605. Conv to Sea Hurricane Mk I.
Z4616, 4619, 4621. Conv to Mk I(T). TAC R Mk I.
Z4624. Conv to Sea Hurricane Mk I.
Z4630. Conv to Mk I(T). To ME.
Z4638. Conv to Sea Hurricane Mk I.
Z4644. Conv to Mk I(T). To ME.
Z4646. Gloster A/Ct. Trials at B Down of tropical filter. Conv to Sea Hurricane Mk I by Gen A/Ct.
Z4649. Conv to Sea Hurricane Mk I
Z4652. Conv to Mk I(T). To ME.

Fourth order for 600 aircraft. Delivered March to September 1941. Serials. Mark I, 150 a/c Z4686-4720, 4760-4809, 4832-4876, 4920-4939. Mark IIA, 39 a/c Z4940-4969, 4987-4989. Mark IIB, 417 a/c Z4990-5006, 5038-5087, 5117-5162, 5202-5236, 5252-5271, 5302-5351, 5376-5395, 5434-5483, 5529-5563, 5580-5629, 5649-5693.

Z4686. Conv to Sea Hurricane Mk I.
Z4689, 4697, 4698, 4700, 4703, 4714, 4718, 4762, 4767. Mk I(T). To ME.
Z770. Gloster A/ct. Trls a/c.
Z4772, 4773, 4775, 4777. Mk I(T). To ME.
K4778. Conv to Sea Hurricane Mk I.
Z4805. Mk I(T). To ME.
Z4809. Farnborough trls of desert paint schemes. To Mk I(T). To ME.
Z4835. Conv to Sea Hurricane Mk I.
K4838. Farnborough. Night fly trials. To B Down.
K4846, 4849, 4851, 4852, 4853, 4854.Conv to Sea

Hurricane Mk I.K4864. Mk I(T). To ME.
K4865. Conv to Sea Hurricane Mk I.K4866. Performance and handling trls B Down. Conv to Sea Hurricane by Gen A/ct.
K4867. Conv to Sea Hurricane Mk I.
K4871. Mk I(T). To Me.
K4873, 4874, 4876, 4920, 4921, 4922, 4923, 4924, 4925, 4926, 4929, 4933. Conv to Sea Hurricane Mk I.
K4934. Mk I(T). To ME.
K4936, 4937, 4938, 4939. Conv to Sea Hurricane Mk I.

Hurricane Mk IIA.

Z4941. Conv to Mk IIB.
Z4942, 4944, 4950, 4952, 4953, 4954, 4955, 4958,

4964. Mk IIA(T). To ME.
Z4948. Mk IIA(T). To ME.

Hurricane Mk IIB.

Z4993. Trials Farnborough.
Z5003. Mk IIB(T).
Z5004, 5005, 5064, 5086, 5087, 5117, 5118, 5132 (mods to PR Mk II), 5137, 5140, 5142, 5143, 5144, 5148. To ME.
Z5210, 5211, 5212, 5213. To Russia.
Z5217. Mk IIB(T).
Z5236, 5259. To Russia.
Z5261. Mk IIB(T) To ME.
Z5262, 5263. To Russia.

Z5306, 5312, 5314, 5330, 5381, 5387, 5388. Mk IIB(T). To ME.
Z5390. Farnborough. Trls a/c.
Z5436, 5443, 5444, 5461. Mk IIB(T). To ME.
Z5480. To Russia.
Z5482. Mk IIB(T). To ME.
Z5529. To Russia.
Z5533, 5587, 5592, 5600, 5604, 5626, 5628, 5659, 5661, 5666, 5668, 5674. Mk IIB(T). To ME.

Hurricane Mk I. (Hawker). 500 aircraft under Contract No. 62305/39. Merlin III. First 25 production fabric wings. Remainder metal. Delivered July 1940 to February 1941. Serials V7200-7209, 7221-7260, 7276-7318, 7337-7386, 7400-7446, 7461-7510, 7533-7572, 7588-7627, 7644-7690, 7705-7737, 7741-7780, 7795-7838, 7851-7862. AS987-990.

V7207, 7229. Conv to Sea Hurricane Mk IA by Gen A/ct.
V7234. Conv to Mk IIA as DG617 by R-R.
V7241, 7244,7246. Conv to Sea Hurricane Mk IA.
V7249. De-icing trials Hawker A/c.
V7252. Conv to Sea Hurricane Mk IA.
V7258. Conv to Mk IIA as DG621 by R-R.
V7260. Trials with 4x20mm cannon at High Alt, B Down.
V7286. Conv to Mk IIA as DR346. To Russia.
V7299, 7300. Mk I(T).
V7301. Conv to Sea Hurricane.
V7302. Conv to Mk IIA as BV164.
V7339. Conv to Sea Hurricane Mk I.
V7349. Conv to Sea Hurricane Mk IA by Gen A/ct.
V7351. Conv to Mk IIA as BV173.
V7352. Conv to Sea Hurricane Mk I by Gen A/ct.
V7354. Mk I(T). To ME.
V7360. Trls 4x20mm cannon wings at B Down.
V7372, 7379. Mk I(T). To ME.
V7379, 7386, 7402. Conv to Sea Hurricane Mk IA by Gen A/ct.
V7411. To Eire 104.
V7416, 7421. Conv to Sea Hurricane Mk IA.
V7423, 7428, 7431. Mk I(T). To ME. To PR Mk I.
V7435. To Eire 112.
V7438, 7439. Conv to Sea Hurricane Mk I.

V7463. To Eire 114.
V7465. Conv to Sea Hurricane Mk I.
V7477, 7479. Mk I(T).
V7480. Trls at B Down. Towed fighter trls with Halifax by Flight Refuelling.
V7482, 7490, 7491, 7492. Mk I(T).
V7498, 7501, 7502, 7503, 7504, 7505, 7506. Conv to Sea Hurricane Mk IA by Gen A/Ct.
V75450. To Eire 105.
V7541, 7542, 7545, 7546, 7547, 7551, 7558, 7559, 7561, 7571. Mk I(T). To ME.
V7588, 7600, 7623, 7646, 7647, 7650. Conv to Sea Hurricane Mk IA.
V7654. Mk I(T). To ME.
V7657. Conv to Mk IIA as DG651 by R-R.
V7665. Conv to Sea Hurricane Mk IA.
V7670. Mk I(T). To ME.
V7681. Conv to Sea Hurricane Mk IA.
V7684. Conv to Mk IIA as DG645 by R-R.
V7685. Conv to Sea Hurricane Mk IA.
V7716, 7617. Mk I(T). To ME.
V7745. Conv to Sea Hurricane Mk I.
V7753, 7757, 7763, 7770, 7772, 7777, 7817, 7820, 7822. Mk I(T). To ME.
V7824. Conv to Sea Hurricane Mk IA.
V7828. Mk I(T). To ME.
AS987, 990. Mk I(T). To ME.

Hurricane Mk IIA, IIB, IIC. (Hawker). 1,000 aircraft under Contract No. 62305/39. Merlin XX. Delivered January to July 1941. Serials. Z2308-2357, 2382-2426, 2446-2465, 2479-2528, 2560-2594, 2624-2643, 2661-2705, 2741-2775, 2791-2840, 2882-2931, 2259-2999, 3017-3036, 3050-3099, 3143-3187, 3221-3276, 3310-3359, 3385-3404, 3421-3470, 3489-3523, 3554-3598, 3642-3691, 3740-3784, 3826-3845, 3885-3919, 3969-4018.

Z2308. Mk IIA. Air intake and performance trials.
Z2314. Mk II(T).
Z2317. Mk IIA.
Z2320/G. Mk IIA. Armament trials B Down.
Z2326/G. Mk IIA. Armament trials with R-R BF and Vickers S, 40mm guns at B Down.
Z2328. Mk IIA(T) To PR Mk IIA.
Z2334, 2340 (Spares a/c), 2341, 2342, 2343. Mk IIA.
Z2346. Cockpit htng trials B Down.
Z2347, 2349, 2351. Mk IIA.
Z2353, 2355, 2383. Mk IIB.
Z2384, 2386, 2388, 2390, 2391. Mk IIA.
Z2396. Mk IIB.
Z2399. Trials with mod oil cooler, Hawker A/ct.
Z2401, 2405. Mk IIB.
Z2410. Mk IIA.
Z2414. M k IIB(T).
Z2415. IIB(T). H/A trls Hawker A/Ct.
Z2416. Mk IIB(T).
Z2446, 2448, 2449, 2454, 2455. Mk IIA.

Z2457. Mk IIA. Farnborough trls a/c.
Z2459. Mk IIA.
Z2461. Mk IIA. Hood jettison trls B Down.
Z2462, 2463, 2482, 2484, 2485, 2488, 2489, 2501, 2502, 2505. Mk IIA.
Z2509, 2513, 2515. Mk IIB(T).
Z2521, 2522. Mk IIA.
Z2565, 2567. Mk IIB.
Z2570, 2572. Mk IIA.
Z2573. Mk IIA. Conv to Mk IIB(T).
Z2575, 2578,2579. Mk IIA.
Z2582. Mk IIB.
Z2585, 2586, 2587. Mk IIA.
Z2589. 4x20mm cannon wing.
Z2591. Mk IIA. Farnborough trls.
Z2628, 2630. Mk IIA.
Z2632, 2633. Mk IIB.
Z2636, 2637, 2639, 2640 (conv to Mk IIB(T)), 2663, 2664, 2667, 2670, 2671, 2674, 2676, Z2677. Mk IIA.
Z2679. Mk IIB(T).

Z2682, 2683, 2684. Mk IIB.
Z2687, 2688, 2689, 2690, 2693, 2696, 2697, 2700, 2702, 2703, 2705, 2744. Mk IIA.
Z2747. Mk IIB.
Z2752, 2755, 2758, 2759, 2763, 2764, 2767, 2769, 2770, 2772, 2774, 2792. Mk IIA.
Z2795. Radio trials at TRE Malvern.
Z2799, 2801, 2802, 2804, 2806, 2807, 2808, 2810, 2814. Mk IIA.
Z2815. Mk IIA(T).
Z2821. Mk IIA.
Z2825. Mk IIA(T).
Z2828. Mk IIA.
Z2832. Mk IIA. Eire 94. Returned to RAF July '43.
Z2884. Mk IIA.
Z2885. Mk IIC. 4x20mm cannon in 'C' wing. B Down trls.
Z2890. Mk IIC. To Turbinlite Sqdn.
Z2891, 2893. Mk IIB.
Z2895. Trials of mod fuel system at B Down.
Z2903. Mk IIB.
Z2905. Trials of 90gal o/load fuel tank, IIC wing, B Down.
Z2906, 2907, 2909, 2916, 2918, 2920, 2926. Mk IIB.
Z2928. Mk IIA.
Z2960. Mk IIB.
Z2961. Mk IIB(T).
Z2962, 2966, 2967. Mk IIA.
Z2985. Mk IIC.
Z2987, 2991, 2992, 3018, 3022, 3025, 3030, 3031, 3036. Mk IIB.
Z3051, 3056, 3058. Mk IIC.
Z3067. Mk IIB.
Z3069, 3070. Mk IIC.
Z3075, 3076, 3078, 3081. Mk IIB.
Z3084, 3086, 3088. Mk IIC.
Z3091. Mk IIB.
Z3092/G. Trls with 3in RPs, B Down
Z3095. Mk IIA.
Z3099. Mk IIB.
Z3148. Mk IIA.
Z3150, 3151, 3156. Mk IIB.
Z3157. Trls with 8/12 gun wing, B Down.
Z3160. Mk IIB.
Z3161. Mk IIB. Conv to Mk IIC. To Turbinlite Sqdn.
Z3164, 3165, 3171. Mk IIB.
Z3165. Mk IIC.
Z3176, 3177. Mk IIA.
Z3179. Gloster A/ct. Trials a/c.
Z3182, 3222, 3225, 3227. Mk IIB.
Z3230. Mk IIA.
Z3238, 3241, 3249, 3257. Mk IIB.

Z3261. Mk IIC.
Z3262, 3263. Mk IIB.
Z3265, 3271. Mk IIC.
Z3314, 3316, 3319, 3322. Mk IIB.
Z3323. Mk IIC.
Z3324, 3332, 3341. Mk IIB.
Z3345, 3347. Mk IIA. Z3353, 3354, 3355, 3356, 3387, 3390, 3395, 3397, 3399, 3402, 3429, 3442, 3447, 3448. Mk IIB.
Z3451. T.I at B Down.
Z3454. Mk IIB.
Z3458. Mk IIA.
Z3465, 3467. Mk IIC.
Z3496, 3521. Mk IIB.
Z3502. Mk IIC.
Z3511, 3513, 3514 (IIB(T)), 3516. Mk IIB.
V3554. IIC(T).
Z3559. Mk IIB.
Z3564. Armament trls with Mk IIB wing, B Down.
Z3573. Mk IIB.
Z3582. Spares a/ct for LF363.
Z3589. Mk IIB.
Z3590. Mk IIC(T).
Z3593, 3595, 3596, 3654, 3659, 3662, 3665, 3668, 3669, 3670, 3672, 3675. Mk IIB.
Z3677. Mk IIA.
Z3684. IIB. Conv to Mk IIC.
Z3686. Mk IIB.
Z3687. Tests with lmainar flow wing, Farnborough.
Z3740, 3744, 3745, 3746 (Russia). Mk IIB.
Z3748. Mk IIC.
Z3760, 3763, 3766, 3768. Mk IIB(T).
Z3770, 3773. Mk IIB.
Z3773, 3774, 3775, 3776. Mk IIC.
Z3779. Mk IIA.
Z3782. Mk IIB.
Z3826, 3830, 3841, 3842, 3930, 3841, 3842, 3843, 3844, 3845, 3885. Mk IIC.
Z3888. Trials with bombs, stores, etc, B Down.
Z3893. Mk IIB. Conv to Mk IIC. To Turbinlite Sqdn.
Z3894, 3897, 3899, 3902, 3903, 3915. Mk IIC.
Z3919. Farnborough, rocket projectile trials.
Z3969. Mk IIB.
Z3970, 3971. Mk IIC.
Z3975, 3976, 3977, 3979. Mk IIB.
Z3981. Performance and handling. Hawker A/ct.
Z3987, 3988. Mk IIB.
Z3992, 4005, 4006, 4007, 4009, 4011, 4014. Mk IIB(T). To ME.
Z4015. Conv to Sea Hurricane Mk IC. Merlin III, 4 cannon wing.
Z4017, 4018. Mk IIB(T). To Russia.

Hurricane Mk I. Canada. Re-designated Mk X. Order I for 20 aircraft. Serials AE958-977. Merlin 28.

AE958, 959. Conv to Sea Hurricane Mk IB.
AE960. Conv to Sea Hurricane Mk IC.
AE961, 962. Conv to Sea Hurricane Mk IB.

AE964. Conv to Sea Hurricane Mk IC.
AE965. Conv to Sea Hurricane Mk IB.
AE966. Conv to Sea Hurricane Mk IC.

AE967, 968, 969. Conv to Sea Hurricane Mk IB. AE972 to 974. Lost at sea.

AE975, 977. Conv to Sea Hurricane Mk IB.

Order II. 300 aircraft. Serials. AF945-AG344.

AF945.946, 947, 949, 950, 951, 952, 953, 954, 955, 961, 962, 963, 965, 967,969,971, 973,974,976,981,982. Conv to Sea Hurricane Mk IB.
AF993. To ME. Rhodesian AF as trainer.
AG101, 106. Mk X.
AG118. Conv to Mk IIC, Merlin XX.
AG119. Mk X. Tac R.
AG122. Conv to Mk IIB.
AG141. Mk X.
AG146, Mk X, unarmed.
AG153. Mk X(T) unarmed.
AG159. Mk X, 12 gun wing.
AG177. Mk X(T).
AG187, 191. Mk X.

AG196. Mk X, 12 gun wing.
AG216. Conv to Mk IB.
AG232. Mk X, 12 gun wing.
AG236. Mk X, 4 cannon wing.
AG237. Mk X.
AG276. Mk X(T).
AG277. Mk X. Conv to Mk IIB.
AG280. Mk X.
AG292. Conv to Mk IIB.
AG299. To RCAF Canada.
AG301. Conv to Mk IIB.
AG310. To RCAF Canada.
AG335. Conv to Sea Hurricane Mk IC.
AG338, 340, 341, 342, 344. Mk X. Conv to Mk IIB.

Order III. Mk IIB. 20 aircraft. Serials AG665-684.

AG665. Evaluation trials, B Down.
AG666, 667. Conv to Mk IIC.

AG672, 673, 674, 675, 676, 677, 678, 679, 680, 681 (lost at sea), 682, 683, 684. To Russia.

Hurricane Mk X. Canada. 100 aircraft, Merlin 28. Serials. AM270-369.

AM270, 271, 272, 275. Conv Mk IIB.
AM279, 280, 281, 283. Conv to Mk IIB.
AM288, 293. Conv to Mk IIC.

AM301, 302. Conv to Mk IIB.
AM311, 315, 347, 349, 358, 367. Conv to Mk IIC.

Hurricane Mk IIB, IIC and IID. (Hawker). 1,350 aircraft. Sixth production batch. Merlin XX. Delivered 24 July 1941 to 18 March 1942. Serials. BD696-745, 759-793, 818-837, 855-899, 914-963, 980-986. BE105-117, 130-174, 193-242, 274-308, 323-372, 394-428, 468-517, 546-590, 632-651, 667-716. RM898-936, 947-996. BN103-142, 155-189, 203-242, 265-298, 311-337, 346-389, 399-435, 449-497, 512-547, 559-603, 624-654, 667-705, 719-759, 773-802, 818-846, 859-882, 896-940, 953-987.

PN696. Mk IIC.
PN697(Russia), 699. Mk IIB.
BD700, 701, 704(Russia), 707, 709, 712, 714. Mk IIB.
BD715. NF IIB. To Turbinlite Sqdn.
BD716. Mk IIB.
BD717. Mk IIB.
BD727. Mk IIB(T).
BD720. NF IIB. To Turbinlite sqdn.
BD727. Mk IIB(T).
BD728, 729. NF IIB. To Turbinlite sqdn.
BD730. Mk IIB(T). To India.
BD731. Mk IIB. To Russia.
BD734, 737, 741. Mk IIB.
BD744. NF IIB.
BD761. NF IIB. To Turbinlite sqdn.
BD764, 765. Mk IIB.
BD766. NF IIB.

BD768. Mk IIB.
BD770. NF IIB. To Turbinlite sqdn.
BD772, 774, 775, 776, 777, 779, 782. Mk IIB(T). To ME.
BD787. Mk IIC.
BD791. Mk IIB(T). To ME.
BD792. Mk IIB(T). To Russia.
BD793. Mk IIB(T). To ME, TAC IIC(T).
BD820. Mk IIB(T).
BD822, 823, 825. Mk IIB. To Russia.
BD831. Mk IIC.
BD833. NF IIC. To Turbinlite sqdn.
BD834, 836, 855, 859, 860, 863. NF IIC
BD866. Mk IIC(T). To ME.
BD867, 868. NF IIC.
BD871. Mk IIC. To Russia.
BD872, 873, 874, 875. Mk IIC.
BD881, 884, 887(T). Mk IIB.

BN471. Mk IIB(T). To ME.
BN481. Mk IIB(T). To Russia.
BN496. Mk IIC(T). To ME.
BN526/G. TI Armament Trls B D.
BN538. Mk IIC(T). To ME.
BN540. Mk IIC(T).
BN560. Mk IIC(T). To ME.
BN564. Mk IIC(T). To India.
BN566. Mk C(T). To ME.
BN569. Mk 11C(T). To India.
BN571/G. T1 Armament Trials B D.
BN581. Mk IIC(T). To India.
BN596. Mk IICT). To India.
BN603. Mk IIC(T). To N.A.
BN627. Mk IIB(T). To N.A.
BN635. Mk IIB(T).

BN649. Mk IIC(T). To ME.
BN672, 676. Mk IIC(T). To India.
BN677. Mk IID(T). To ME.
BN678. Mk IIC(T). To ME.
BN696, 701, 703, 704, 719, 780, 781. Mk IIC(T).
To India.
BN797. Mk IID(T). To NE.
BN826. Mk IIC(T). To ME.
BN837, 841, 842, 845, 846, 860, 861. Mk IID(T).
To ME.
BN868. Mk IIC(T). To India.
BN870. Mk IIC(T). Tac R. To ME.
BN878, 896, 906, 959. Mk IIC(T). To India.
BN960. Mk IIC(T). To ME.
BN961. Mk IID(T). To ME.
BB970. Mk IIC(T).

Hurricane IIA, IIB,IIC (Gloster). 450 A/C. Serials BG674-723, 727-771, 783-832, 844-888, 901-920, 933-977, 990-999. BH115-154, 167-201, 215-264, 277-296, 312-361. Delivered September 1941 to December 1941.

BG675. Mk IIB.
BG688. Mk IIB. To India.
BG689. NF IIB(T). To ME.
BG691. Mk IIA(T). To ME.
BG692. Mk IIA(T).
BG693. Mk IIB. To F.E.
BG697. Mk IIB. To India.
BG705. Mk IIB.
BG707, 745. Mk IIB. To ME.
BG750, 751. Mk IIC(T). To ME.
BG753. Mk IIB. To ME.
BG760. Mk IIB.
BG770, 784. Mk IIB.
BG785. Mk IIA(T). TAC R. To ME.
BG801. Mk IIB.
BG802. Mk IIB(T). TAC R. To India.
BG809, 810, 812, 815, 827, 828. Mk IIB(T).
BG846. Mk IIB. To F.E.
BG854. Mk IIB.
BG857. Mk IIB. To India.
BG858. Mk IIB. To F.E.
BG859. Mk IIB. To ME.
BG864. Mk IIB. To F.E.
BG867. NF IIC(T). To ME.
BG872. Mk IIB.

BG877. NF IIC(T). To ME.
BG887. Mk IIB.
BG902. NF IIC(T). To ME.
BG913, 914, 916, 936. Mk IIB.
BG940. Mk IIB. To ME.
BG942. Mk C(T). To India.
BG946. Mk IIB. To India.
BG949, 950. Mk IIB. To ME.
BG961. Mk IIB. To India.
BG963. Mk IIB.
BG966, 971. Mk IIB. To ME.
BG974. NF IIC(T). To ME.
BG992. Mk IIB(T). Tac R. To ME.
BG994. Mk IIB. To India.
BG998. Mk IIB(T). Tac R. To ME.
BH115. Mk IIB. To India.
BH126. Mk IIB. To N.A.
BH127. Mk IIB.
BH131. Mk IIB. To ME.
BH132. Mk IIB. To India.
BH133. Mk IIB. To ME.
BH135. Mk II1B.
BH151. Mk IIB. To India.
BH217. Mk IIB. To N.A.
BH230. Mk IIB. To India.

Hurricane IIB,IIC,IID. (Hawker). 1,888 aircraft to seventh order. Merlin XX. Serials. BN998-992. BP109-141, 154-200, 217-245, 259-302, 316-362, 378-416, 430-479, 493-526, 538-566, 579-614, 628-675, 692-711, 734-772. HL544-591,603-634,654-683,698-747,763-809,828-867,879-913,925-941, 953-997. HM110-157. HV275-317, 333-370, 396-445, 468-516, 534-560, 577-612, 634-674, 696-745, 768-799, 815-858, 873-921, 943-989. HW115-146, 167-207, 229-278, 291-323, 345-373, 399-444, 467-501, 533-572, 596-624, 651-686, 713-757, 779-808, 834-881. Delivered 17 March 1941 to 23 November 1942.

BP110. Mk IIC(T).
BP123, 126, 127, 128. Mk IIC(T). To ME.
BP131, 136, 157. Mk IID(T). To ME.
BP167. NF IIC(T). To India.
BP173/E11D Arms Trials BD. 29/7/42 conv to
MK V.
BP175. NF IIC(T). To India.
BP177. NF IIC(T). To ME.

BP183. Mk IID(T). To ME.
BP186. NF Mk IIC (T). To ME.
BP187. Mk IIC(T) Bomber.
BP188, 193. MK IID(T). To ME.
BP219. Mk IIC(T). To ME.
BP224. Mk IIC(T). Met To ME.
BP231, 232, 237. MK IIC(T). To ME.
BP240. Mk IIC(T). To India.

BP279, 282. Mk IIB(T). To ME.
BP287. NF Mk IIC(T). To ME.
BP288, 289. Mk IIC(T). To ME.
BP290. Mk IIB(T). To ME.
BP295. Mk IIB Bomber.
BP317. Mk IIB(T). To ME.
BP324. Mk IIB(T) Bomber.
BP329. Mk IIB(T). To ME.
BP337, 340. Mk IIC(T). Tac R. To ME.
BP341, 342. Mk IIC(T). Bomber To ME.
BP344. NF MK IIC(T).
BP346, 348, 358, 359. Mk IIC(T). To ME.
BP380. NF MK IIC(T).
BP381, 384, 387, 389. Mk IIC(T). To ME.
BP391. Mk IIC(T). Met duties ME.
BP397. Mk IIC(T). To ME.
BP398. NF Mk IIC(T). To ME.
BP409, 410. Mk IIC(T). To ME.
BP414. Mk II(T) Tac R.
BP440. Mk IIB(T) Bomber. To ME.
BP442. MK IIB(T). To ME.
BP446. Mk 11C(T). Tac R. To ME.
BP459, 462, 465. Mk IIC(T). To ME.
BP466. NF Mk IIC(T). To ME.
BP467, 468, 469. Mk IIC(T). To ME.
BP470, 471, 472, 473, 510, 512, 515. Mk IIC(T).
To ME.
BP518, 521. NF Mk IIC(T). To ME.
BP541. Mk IIC(T). To ME.
BP550. Mk IID (T) To ME.
BP566. NF Mk IIC(T). To ME.
BP580, 581. Mk IIC(T). To ME.
BP584. NF Mk IIC(T). To ME.
BP585, 586, 592, 593. Mk IIC(T). To ME.
BP604. Mk IIB(T) Bomber. Tac R. To ME.
BP610. Mk B (T). Tac R. To ME.
BP645. Mk IIC(T). To ME.
BP649. NF Mk IIC.
BP653. Mk IIC Bomber.
BP656. Mk IIC(T). To ME.
BP657. NF MK IIC.
BP662. Mk IIC(T) Bomber.
BP666. Mk IIC(T). To ME.
BP668. Mk IIC.
BP672. Mk IIC Bomber.
BP700, 703. Mk IIB
BP704, 706. NF Mk IIC. Turbinlite.
BP734. Mk IIC(T). To ME.
BP737. Mk IIB Bomber.
BP742. Mk IIB (T) Bomber.
BP746. Mk IIC Bomber.
BP756. Mk IIC(T). To India.
BP758. Mk IIB(T). To ME.
BP760. NF MkIIC. Turbinlite.
BP763. Mk IIC(T) Met. To ME.
BP769. NF Mk IIC.
HL560. NF Mk IIC.
HL562. NF Mk IIC. Turbinlite.
HL563. NF Mk IIC.
HL564, 565. Mk IIC(T). To ME.
HL569. Mk IIB(T). To ME.
HL570, 584. NF IIC. Turbinlite.
HL589. NF IIC.

HL603, 604.NF IIC.
HL605. NF Mk IIC. Turbinlite.
HL607, 609, 611. Mk IIC(T). To ME.
HL612. Mk IIB(T). N.A.
HL627. Mk IIC(T). To ME.
HL629. Mk IIB(T). To N.A.
Hl632. Mk IIC(T).
HL654. Mk IIC(T). To ME.
HL656. NF Mk IIC.
HL658, 660. NF Mk IIC. Turbinlite.
HL664. NF Mk IIC(T). To ME.
HL665. Mk IIC Bomber. To Russia.
HL669. NF Mk IIC.
HL678. NF Mk IIC(T) TAC R. To ME.
HL683. Mk IIC(T). To ME.
HL699. IIB(T). To ME.
HL700. IIC(T). To ME.
HL701. IIC(T) Bomber.
HL705. IIB Bomber.
HL707. NF IIB(T). To Me.
HL715, 716. IIB Bomber.
HL721. IIC(T). To Me.
HL723, 728. IIB Bomber.
HL733. IIB(T) Bomber. To ME.
HL735, 737. IIC(T). To ME.
HL739. IIB(T). TAC R. To ME.
HL772. IIB(T).
HL773. IIC(T).
HL779. NF IIB(T). To ME.
HL783. IIB(T). To FE.
HL785. IIB(T). To ME.
HL790. IIC(T) Met. To ME.
HL791. IIB(T). To India.
HL795. IIC(T). Bomber. To ME.
HL796. NF IIC(T). To ME.
HL797. Mk IIC(T). To ME.
HL799. NF Mk IIC(T). To ME.
HL800. Mk IIC(T). Tac R. To N.A.
HL801. NF Mk IIC(T). To ME.
HL802. NF Mk IIB(T). To India.
HL804. Mk IIB(T).
HL805. Mk IIC(T). To ME.
HL830. Mk IIC(T) Tac R. To ME.
HL831. NF Mk II(T). To ME.
HL832,833.Mk IIC(T). To ME.
I IL834. Mk IIB(T). To ME.
HL838. Mk IIC(T). To ME.
HL839,841. NF Mk IIC(T). To ME.
HL844,846. Mk IIC(T). To ME.
HL849. MkIIC(T). Tac R. To ME.
HL851. Mk IIC(T). To ME.
HL852. NF Mk IIC(T). To ME.
HL855. Mk IIC(T) Tac R. To ME.
HL857. Mk IIB(T). To India.
HL859, 861, 862, 863. NF Mk IIC.
HL864. NF Mk IIC(T). To N.A.
HL867. Mk IIB(T). To India.
HL884. Mk IIC(T). To ME.
HL886. Mk IIC(T). To India.
HL887, 891, 892, 900, 901, 904, 905, 907. Mk
IIC(T). To ME.
HL925. Mk IIC(T) Bomber. To ME.
HL926. Mk IIC(T). To ME.

HL933. NF Mk IIC(T) To ME.
HL941. Mk IIC(T). To ME.
HL956, 958, 965, 991, 994, 995. NF Mk IIC(T).
To ME.
HM110. Mk IIC(T). To India.
HM111. Mk IIB(T). To ME.
HM114, 118. Mk IIC(T). To ME.
HM123. Mk IIB(T).
HM131. Mk IIC(T). To ME.
HM133. Mk IIB(T). To India.
HM135, 136. NF Mk IIC(T). To ME.
HM139. Mk IIC(T). To India.
HM145. Mk IIC(T). To ME.
HV288, 290, 294. Mk IIC(T). To ME.
HV295. MkIIB(T). To ME.
HV297. Mk IIB(T) Bomber. To ME.
HV299. NF Mk IIC(T). To ME.
HV305, 314, 315. Mk IIC(T). To ME.
HV317. NF Mk IIC(T). To ME.
HV334, 335, 336, 350, 352, 357, 360. Mk IIC(T).
To ME.
HV363. Mk IIB Bomber.
HV366. Mk IIC(T).
HV370. Mk IIC(T) Met. To N.A.
HV399. Mk IIC(T). To ME.
HV400. NF Mk IIC(T). To ME.
HV402, 403. Mk IIC(T). To ME.
HV405. Mk IIC(T) Tac R. To India.
HV406, 407, 408, 409. Mk IIC(T). To ME.
HV412. Mk IIC(T). To India.
HV417, 421. MkIIC(T). To ME.
HV422. Mk IIB(T). To India.
HV426. Mk IIC(T). To ME.
HV427. Mk IIC(T). To India.
HV428. Mk IIB(T). To India.
HV437. Mk IIB(T) Bomber. To India.
HV440. Mk IIC(T). To ME.
HV441. Mk IIC(T) Bomber. To ME.
HV468. Mk IIC(T). To ME.
HV473. Mk IIC(T). To India.
HV474. Mk IIC(T). To ME.
HV475. Mk IIB(T). Bomber.
HV479. Mk IIC(T) PR. To ME.
HV480. Mk IIB(T) Bomber. To ME.
HV483, 484. Mk IIC(T). To ME.
HV490. Mk IIB(T) Bomber. To ME.
HV493. Mk IIB(T) Bomber.
HV497. Mk IIB(T). To India.
HV500. Mk IIC(T) Met. To N E A.
HV502. Mk IIB(T) Bomber. To India.
HV505. Mk IIB(T) Bomber.
HV511. Mk IIC(T). To ME.
HV513. Mk IIC(T). To Turkey.
HV516. Mk IIC(T) Bomber. To ME.
HV536, 539, 540, 541. Mk IIC(T). To ME.
HV542. Mk IIC(T) Bomber. To ME.
HV546. Mk IIC(T). To FE.
HV548. Mk IIC(T) Bomber. To ME.
HV551. Mk IIC(T). To Turkey.
HV555. Mk IIB(T) Bomber.
HV559, 579. Mk IIB(T) Bomber. To India.
HV580. Mk IIC(T). To N.A.
HV583. Mk IIC(T) Met. To N.E.A.

HV585. NF Mk IIC(T) Bomber. To ME.
I IV587. Mk IIC(T) Bomber. To ME.
HV594. Mk IID(T). To ME.
HV608. Mk IIC(T) Met. To N.E.A.
HV609. Mk IIC(T). To ME.
HV635, 636, 640, 644. Mk IIC(T). To India.
HV652. Mk IIB Bomber. To India.
HV660. Mk IIB Bomber. To Persia.
HV661. Mk IIC(T) Bomber. To N.E.A.
HV662. Mk IIC(T) Bomber. To FE.
HV663. Mk IID(T). To E.A.
HV664. Mk IIB(T). To E.A.
HV666. Mk IIC(T). To ME.
HV669. Mk IID(T). To ME.
HV696. Mk IIC(T). To N.E.A.
HV710. NF MkIIC(T) Tac R.To FE.
HV711. Mk IIC(T) Met. To ME.
HV712. Mk IIC(T). To ME.
HV714. Mk IIB Bomber. To ME.
HV718. Mk IIC(T). To N.E.A.
HV722. Mk IIC(T).
I IV723. Mk IIC(T). To India.
HV735. Mk IIC(T). To Persia.
HV739. Mk IIC(T) Bomber. To India.
HV740, 742. Mk IIC(T). To ME.
HV743, 744. Mk IIC(T). To India.
HV745. Mk IIC(T). To ME.
HV780. Mk IIC(T) Met. To N.E.A.
HV783. Mk IIC(T). To India.
HV785. Mk IIC(T). To N.A.
HV786. Mk IIB(T). To India.
HV793. Mk IIC(T) Bomber. To FF.
HV796, 798, 815. Mk IIC(T). To India.
HV817. Mk IIC(T). To N.E.A.
HV818. NF Mk IIC(T). To ME.
HV828. NF Mk IIC(T). To India.
HV830. Mk IIC(T). To ME.
HV834. Mk IIC(T). To Persia.
HV836. Mk IIB Bomber. To India.
HV838, 843. Mk IIC(T). To ME.
HV844, 884. Mk IIB Bomber.
HV887. Mk IIC(T). To India.
HV890. Mk IIC(T) Met. To ME.
HV891, 901. Mk IIC(T). To N.A.
I IV902. Mk IIC(T). To N E A.
HV911. Mk IIB(T) Bomber. To ME.
HV947. Mk IIC Bomber. To India.
HV953. Mk IIC(T). To ME.
HV956. Mk IIC(T). To India.
HV958. Mk IIC(T). To ME.
HV967. Mk IIC Bomber. To FE.
HV970. Mk IIC(T). To N.E.A.
HV973. NF Mk IIC.
HV983. Mk IIB Bomber. To India.
HV984, 985. Mk IIC(T). To ME.
HV988. Mk IIC(T). To N.E.A.
HW115. Trials Prod Oil System.
HW116. NF Mk IIC(T). To ME.
HW118. Mk IIB Bomber.
HW121. Mk IIC(T). To N.E.A.
HW122, 128. Mk IIC(T). To ME.
HW129, 130, 131. NF Mk IIC Turbinlite.
HW137. Mk IIC(T). To N.E.A.

HW140. Mk IIB Bomber.
HW167. Mk IIB(T). To N.E.A.
HW168. Mk IIC(T). To N.E.A.
HW173. Mk IIB(T). To ME.
HW178. Mk IIB(T) Bomber. To ME.
HW182/G. B Down Arms Trls.
HW183. Mk IIC(T). To N.A.
HW187/G. B Down Arms Trls.
HW189, 194, 197. Mk IIC(T). To ME.
HW199. Mk IIC(T). To India.
HW203. Trials drop tanks on 'U' wing.
HW204. Mk IIC(T). To N A.
HW206, 207. Mk IIC. No Guns.
HW235. Mk IIC(T). To ME.
HW239. Mk IIC(T). To N.A.
HW242. NF Mk IIC. To ME.
HW247. Mk IIC(T). To ME.
HW257. Mk IIC(T). To N.A.
HW267, 270. Mk IIB(T). To India.
HW271, 298, 303, 323, 359. Mk IID(T). To ME.
HW361. Mk IIC(T). To ME.
HW371. Mk IIB(T). To India.
HW404. Mk IIC(T). To ME.
HW407. Mk IIC(T). To India.
HW413. NF Mk IIC(T). To ME.
HW415. NF Mk IIC(T). To India.
HW421. Mk IIC(T). To N.A.
HW423. Mk IIC(T). To FE.
HW431, 432. NF Mk IIC.
HW433. Mk IIC(T). To ME.
HW435. Mk IIC(T). To India.
HW436, 437. Mk IIC(T). To N.A.
HW438. Mk IID(T). To India.
HW439. Mk IID(T). To ME.
HW443. Mk IIC(T). To N.A.

HW474, 483. Mk IIC(T). To ME.
HW485. NF MkIIC.
HW489. Mk IIB (T) Bomber. To India.
HW538. Mk IIC(T). To ME.
HW539. Mk IIC(T) Tac R. To India.
HW551. NF Mk IIC Turbinlite.
HW554. NF Mk IIC Turbinlite.
HW558. Mk IIC(T) Bomber. To India.
HW561. Mk IIC(T). To N.A.
HW569. Mk IIC(T). To N.E.A.
HW571. Mk IIC(T). To ME.
HW602. Mk IIC(T) Bomber. To FE.
HW608. Mk IIC(T). To ME.
HW619. Mk IIC(T). To N.A.
HW655, 660. Mk IIC(T). To India.
HW663. Mk IIC(T) PR. To ME.
HW660. Mk IIC(T) Bomber. To India.
HW663. Mk IIC(T) PR. To ME.
HW666. Mk IIC(T). To India.
HW673. Mk IID(T). To India.
HW684, 716, 719, 723, 728. Mk IID 40mm A/T Guns.
HW737, 738. Mk IIC(T). To ME.
HW747. Arms Trials B Down.
HW756. Mk IIC(T). To FE.
HW794. Mk IIC(T). To India.
HW800. Mk IIC(T). To ME.
HW803. Mk IIC(T). To India.
HW808. Mk IIC(T). To FE.
HW848. NF Mk IIC(T). To ME.
HW855, 857, 859. Mk IIC(T). To India.
HW862. Mk IID(T). To India.
HW868. Mk IIC(T). To N.A.
HW871. Mk IIC(T) Bomber. To FE.
HW878. Mk IID(T). To India.

Hurricane IIB, IIC, IID & IV. 1,200 a/c under Contract No.62305/39/C. Delivered 20 November 1942 to 19 April '43. Serials KW745-777, 791-832, 846-881, 893-936, 949-982. KX101-146, 161-202, 220-261, 280-307, 321-369, 382-425, 452-491, 521-567, 579-621, 691-736, 749-784, 796-838, 851-892, 922-967, K2111-156, 169-201, 218-250, 266-301, 319-356, 370-412, 424-470, 483-526, 540-582, 597-612.

KW697. Mk IIC(T) Bomber. To ME.
KW699. Mk IIB(T). To India.
KW705. Mk IIB(T). To N.A.
KW709, 714. Mk IIB(T). To FE.
KW716. Mk IID(T). To Italy.
KW719. Mk IIC(T). To India.
KW720. Mk IID(T). To India.
KW752. Mk IIC Bomber.
KW756. Mk IIC(T) Bomber. To ME.
KW770. Mk IIC(T) Bomber. Conv to Sea Hurricane as NF668 Mk IIC.
KW774. Mk IIC(T) Bomber To FE.
KW791. Mk IIC(T) Bomber.
KW792. Mk IIC. Conv to Sea Hurricane as NF670.
KW794. Mk IID(T). To India.
KW796. Mk IIC(T). To FE.
KW797. Mk IID(T). To India.
KW799. To Sea Hurricane as NF672.
KW800. Mk IV.
KW801. Mk IIC(T) Bomber. To India.

KW804. To Sea Hurr Mk IIC NF 674.
KW808. To Sea Hurr Mk IIC NF675.
KW809. To Sea Hurr Mk IIC NF678.
KW810. MkIV.
KW816. To Sea Hurr Mk IIC NF679.
KW817. To Sea Hurr Mk IIC NF680.
KW818, 827, 828, 829. Mk IIC(T) Bomber. To India.
KW830. Mk IIC(T) Bomber. To N.A.
KW849. Sea Hurricane Mk IIC NF683.
KW850. Sea Hurricane Mk IIC NF684.
KW860. Sea Hurricane Mk IIC NF685.
KW862. Sea Hurricane Mk IIC NF686.
KW863. Mk IID(T). To India.
KW864. Mk IIC(T) Bomber. To ME.
KW865. Mk IID(T). To India.
KW866. Mk IIC(T) Bomber. To FE.
KW868. Sea Hurricane Mk IIC NF687.
KW870. Sea I Hurricane Mk IIC NF688.
KW878. Sea Hurricane Mk IIC NF689.
KW880. Sea Hurricane Mk IIC NF690.

KW897. Mk IV(T). To India.
KW898. Mk IID(T). To India
KW899. Sea Hurricane Mk IIC NF692.
KW908. Sea Hurricane Mk IIC NF693.
KW910. Mk IV. To India.
KW911. Mk IV.
KW915. Mk IIC(T) Bomber. To ME.
KW918. Mk IV 40mm A/T Guns.
KW919. NF Mk IV.
KW920. Sea Hurricane Mk IIC NF699.
KW921. Sea Hurricane Mk IIC NF700.
KW926. Mk IIC(T) Bomber. To N.A.
KW928. Sea Hurricane Mk IIC NF701.
KW928. Sea Hurricane Mk IIC NF702.
KW930. Sea Hurricane Mk IIC NF703.
KW93, 935, 950. Mk IIC(T) Bomber. To ME.
KW965, 981. Mk IIC(T) Bomber. To N.A.
KX106. Mk IIC(T) Bomber. To India.
KX121. Mk IID(T). To India.
KX125. Mk IIC(T) Bomber. To Russia.
KX127. Mk IIC(T) Bomber. To India.
IOX142. Mk IID Anti tank trials
KX146. Mk IIC(T) Bomber. To N.A.
KX177. Mk IID(T). To Russia.
KX178. Mk IV. To Italy.
KX180. Mk IV. Trials B Down.
KX229, 247. Mk IID(T). To India.
KX249. Mk IID(T) 40mm Guns. To India.
KX304. Mk IID.
KX359. Mk IIC(T) Bomber. To India.
KX401. Mk IIC Bomber.
KX405. Mk IV Conv to Mk V. Prod Trls B Down. Conv to Mk IV.
KX407, 409. Mk IIC Bomber.
KX412. Mk IIC Bomber. Comp trls with KX405 HAL.
KX413, 525. Mk IIC Bomber.
KX536, 540,541,542. Mk IV RPs only.
KX561. Mk IIC Bomber.
KX580, 582, 584, 585. Mk IV RPs only.
KX596. Mk IIC Bomber.
KX605. Mk IIC(T) Bomber. To India.
KX696. Mk IIC Bomber.
KX697. Mk IV RPs only.
KX701. Mk IV Trainer.
KX702. Mk IV RPs only.
KX754. Mk IIC(T) Bomber.
KX800. Mk IV(T) RPs only. To Yugoslavia.
KX802. Mk IV(T). To India.
KX805. Mk IV(T) 40mm Guns.
KX807. Mk IV(T) RPs only.
KX813. Mk IIC(T) Bomber.
KX826. Mk IV 40mm Guns. To Italy.
KX827, 829. Mk IV 40mm Guns.
KX835, 838. Mk IIC(T) Bomber. To ME.
KX862. Mk IV. TI. B Down.
KX863. Mk IIC(T) Bomber. To India.
KX865. Mk IID(T). To Russia.
KX869. Mk IIC(T) Bomber.
KX876. Mk IV(T) 40mm. To Italy.
KX877. Mk IV(T) Conv to Mk V, Merlin 32. Trls B Down.
KX879. Mk IV RPs only.
KX881. Mk IV(T) RPs only. To Yugoslavia.

KX882. Mk IV(T) RPs only.
KX885. Mk IV(T) 40mm. To Italy.
KX886. Mk IIC(T).
KX888. Mk IIC Bomber. To Italy.
KX889. Mk IIC(T) Bomber. To India.
KX927, 932, 936. Mk IIC(T) Bomber. To ME.
KX938. Mk IIC(T) Bomber. To Yugoslavia.
KX951. Mk IIC(T) Bomber. To India.
KX954. Mk IIC(T) Bomber. To ME.
KX957. Mk IIC(T) Bomber. To India.
KX963, 967. Mk IIC(T) Bomber. To ME.
KZ111. Mk IIC(T) Bomber. To Italy.
KZ113. Mk IIC(T) Bomber.
KZ114, 115, 118. Mk IIC(T) Bomber. To ME.
KZ126. Mk IIC(T) Bomber. To India.
KZ130. Mk IIC(T) Bomber. To ME.
KZ138. Mk IIC(T) Bomber. To N.A.
KZ142, 144. MkIIC(T) Bomber .To ME.
KZ185. Mk IV 40mm Guns.
KZ187, 188. Mk IV(T) 40mm Guns. To Italy.
KZ189. Mk IV(T) 40mm Guns
KZ190. Mk IV A/A Duties
KZ193. Mk V. Trls conv to IV 40mm Guns.
KZ194. Mk IV 40mm Guns.
KZ218. Mk IIC(T) Bomber. To India.
KZ222. Mk IV RPs only.
KZ228. MkIV 40mm Guns.
KZ232. Mk IIC Bomber. Trls B Down.
KZ299. Mk IIC(T) Bomber. To India.
KZ301. Mk IV(T) 40mm Guns. To Russia.
KZ321. Mk IV(T) 40mm Guns. To Italy.
KZ325. Mk IV A/A Duties.
KZ335. Mk IIC(T) Bomber. To ME.
KZ352, 356. Mk IIC(T) Bomber. To India.
KZ378. Mk IV RPs only.
KZ382. Mk IV(T) RPs only. To Yugoslavia.
KZ396. Mk IV(T) RPs only.
KZ397. Mk IV(T) 40mm Guns RPs. To ME.
KZ398. Mk IV RPs only.
KZ399. Mk IV RPs only.
KZ400. Mk IV RPs only.
KZ405. Mk IVC Bomber.
KZ406. Mk IV 40mm guns.
KZ435. Mk IIC(T) Bomber. To ME.
KZ446. Mk IIC(T) Bomber. To ME.
KZ448. MK IIC(T) Bomber.
KZ449. Mk IIC Bomber. To Yugoslavia.
KZ460. Mk IIC(T) Bomber. To India.
KZ465. Mk IIC(T) Bomber. To ME.
KZ466. Mk IIC(T) Bomber. Trials HAL.
KZ488. Mk IIC(T) Bomber. To Italy.
KZ497. Mk IIC(T) Bomber. To India.
KZ513. Mk IIC(T) Bomber. To ME.
KZ520. Mk IIC(T) Bomber. To India.
KZ526, 543. Mk IIC(T) Bomber. To India.
KZ550. Mk IV(T) Bomber. To India.
KZ552. Mk IV RPs only.
KZ553. Mk IV 40mm guns. To Italy.
KZ554. Mk IV RPs only.
KZ569. Mk IIC(T) Bomber. To Inda.
KZ571. Mk IV A.S.R. Missions.
KZ572, 576, 579, 606, 607, 609, 611. Mk IV RPs only.

Hurricane Mk IIC, IV (Hawker). 1,205 a/c under Contract No. 62305/39/C Delivered 18 April 1940 to 29 September 1943, Serials KZ613-632, 646-689, 702-750, 766-801, 817-862, 877-920, 933-949. LA101-144. LB542-913, 927-973, 986-999. LD100-131, 157-185, 199-219, 232-266, 287-315, 334-351, 369-416, 435-470, 487-508, 524-509, 557-580, 594-632, 651-695, 723-749, 772-809, 827-866, 885-905, 931-979, 993-999.

KZ620. Mk IV RPs only.
KZ622, 629. Mk IIC(T) Bomber. To ME.
KZ647. Mk IIC(T). To Tac R. To India.
KZ655, 661, 662. Mk IV 40mm guns.
KZ669. Mk IIC(T) Bomber. To Italy.
KZ674, 676, 678. Mk IV RPs only.
KZ679/G. Mk IV RPs only. RP trls B Down.
KZ735. Mk IIC(T) Bomber. To ME.
KZ742. Mk IIC(T) Bomber. To India.
KZ745, 770. Mk IIC(T) Bomber. To India.
KZ784. Mk IIC(T) Bomber. To ME.
KZ785. Mk IIC(T) Bomber. To India.
KZ794. Mk IIC(T) Bomber. To ME.
KZ818 Mk IIC(T) Bomber. To N.A.
KZ827, 829. Mk IV 40mm guns.
KZ831. Mk IIC(T) Bomber. To India.
KZ888. Mk IIC(T) Bomber. To Burma.
KZ893. Mk IIC(T) Bomber. To ME.
KZ894. Mk IIC(T) Bomber. To India.
KZ896. Mk IIC(T) Bomber. To ME.
KZ906. Mk IV RPs only.
KZ909. Mk IV(T) Bomber. To India.
KZ912. Mk IV RPs only.
KZ917. Mk IIC(T) Bomber. To India.
KZ918. Mk IV 40mm Guns.
KZ934, 935, 940, 943. Mk IIC(T) Bomber. To India.
LA108, 111, 119, 124, 129, 131, 140. Mk IIC(T) Bomber. To India.
LB545. Mk IIC(T) Bomber. To India.
LB551. Mk IIC(T) Bomber. Conv To Mk IIB(T). To India.
LB557, 569. Mk IIC(T) Bomber. To India.
LB602. Mk IIC(T) Bomber. To I.A.F.
LB615. Mk IIC(T) Tac R. To India.
LB618, 619. Mk IIC(T) Bomber. To India.
LB648. Mk IV(T) Bomber. To India.
LB649. Mk IV(T) RPs only. To Italy.
LB650. Mk IV No Arms. A/A Duties.
LB658. Mk IIC(T) Bomber.
LB664. Mk IIC(T) Bomber. To I.A.F.
LB672. Mk IIC(T) Bomber. To India.
LB675. Mk IIC(T) Bomber. To ME.
LB677. NF Mk IIC(T) Bomber. To ME.
LB683. Mk IV(T) RPs only. To Italy.
LB718. Mk IIC(T). To India.
LB727. Mk IIC(T) Bomber. To India.
LB732. Mk IIC(T) Bomber. To I.A.F.
LB734. Mk IIC(T) Bomber. To India.
LB740. Mk IIC(T) Bomber. To India.
LB771. Mk IV. To 4628M.
LB774. Mk IV(T) RPs only. To Italy.
LB776. Mk IV(T) Bomber. To India.
LB790. Mk IIC(T) Bomber. To India.
LB795. Mk IIC(T) Bomber. To ME.
LB833, 848. Mk IIC(T) Bomber. To India.
LB852. Mk IV(T) Bomber. To India.

LB854. Mk IIC(T) Bomber. To India.
LB857, 875, 876, 879, 880, 883, 885. Mk IIC(T) Bomber. To India.
LB891, 893. Mk IIC TT. No guns.
LB931, 932, 935. Mk IIC(T) Bomber. To India
LB938, 939. Mk IIC(T) Bomber. To ME.
LB957. Mk IIC(T) Bomber. To India.
LB966. Mk IIC(T) Bomber. To Italy.
LB990. Mk IIC(T) Bomber. To Burma.
LB991. Mk IIC(T) Tac R. To Russia.
LB995. Mk IV RPs only. To Italy.
LB999. Mk IV Bomber. To India.
LD101. Mk IV Bomber. To India.
LD107. Mk IIC(T) Bomber. To Burma.
LD122. Mk IIC(T) Tac R. To India.
LD162. Mk IV RPs only. To Italy.
LD163. Mk IV(T). To India.
LD168. Mk IV(T) RPs only. To Italy.
LD172. Mk IIC(T) Bomber. To Burma.
LD182. Mk IIC Bomber. Written off.
LD185. Mk IIC(T) Bomber. To Burma.
LD206. Mk IIC(T) Bomber. To Burma.
LD215. Mk IIC(T) Tac R. To India.
LD237. Mk IV(T) Bomber. To India.
LD264. Mk IIC Bomber. Arms trials B Down.
LD265. Mk IIC Bomber. To Burma.
LD293. Mk IV(T) 40mm Guns. To Burma.
LD294. Mk IV(T) Bomber. To India.
LD299. Mk IIC(T) Tac R. To India.
LD300. Mk IIC(T) Tac R. To Burma.
LD346. Mk IIC(T). To Burma.
LD387. Mk IIC(T) Tac R. To India.
LD395. Mk IIC(T) Bomber. To India.
LD403, 404. Mk IIC(T) Bomber. To Burma.
LD412. Mk IIC(T) Bomber. To India.
LD438, 439 Mk IIC Bomber. Arms trials B. Down.
LD442. Mk IV(T) Bomber. To India.
LD447. Mk IV(T) 40mm Guns. To Burma.
LD453. Mk IIC(T) Bomber. To India.
LD564, 570. Mk IV RPs only.
LD571, 605. Mk IV(T) Bomber. To India.
LD621. Mk IIC(T) Bomber.
LD627, 675. Mk IIC(T) Bomber. To India.
LD726. Mk IIC(T) Bomber. To Burma.
LD774, 780, 798. Mk IIC(T) Bomber. To India.
LD859. Mk IIC(T) Bomber. To Burma.
LD865. Mk IV(T) RPs only. To Italy.
LD890. Mk IIC(T) Bomber. To India.
LD964. Mk IIC(T) Bomber. To Burma.
LD972, 973. Mk IV RPs only.
LD975. Mk IV(T) RPs only. To Italy.
LD976. Mk IV Conv To TT. A/A Duties.
LD977. Mk IV No arms.
LD997. Mk II(T) Tal R. To India.
LD998. Mk II(T) Bomber. To Burma.

Hurricane. IIB, IIC, IV.(Hawker). Tenth order of 1,357 under Contract No. 62305/39/C. Merlin XX, 24 or 27 engines. 143 Mk IVs cancelled 1 December 1943. Delivered 29 September 1943 to 24 May 1944. Serials LE121-146, 163-183, 201-214, 247-273, 291-309, 334-368, 387-405, 432-449, 456-484, 499-535, 552-593, 617-665, 679-713, 737-769, 784-816, 829-867, 885-925, 938-966, 979-999. LF101-153, 158-184, 197-237, 256-298, 313-346, 359-405, 418-435, 451-482, 494-516, 529-542, 559-601, 620-660, 674-721, 737, 774. MW335-373. PG425-456, 469-499, 512-554, 567-610. PZ730-778, 791-835, 848-865.

LE166. Mk IIC(T) Bomber. To Burma.
LE181. Mk IIC TT. To India.
LE248, 263. Mk IIC Bomber. To Burma.
LE836, 839 Mk IV. No arms. A/A duties.
LE991. Mk IIC Bomber. To Burma.
LE993, 999. Mk IIC Bomber.
LF113. Mk IV(T) 40mm guns. To India.
LF118. Mk IIC Fighter.
LF133. Mk IIC Bomber. Sold Portugal.
LF156. Mk IIC Bomber. To Burma.
LF157. Mk IIC(T) Bomber. To India.
LF160. Mk IIC Bomber.
LF167. Mk IIC(T) Bomber. To Burma.
LF180. Mk IIC. Bomber.
LF197. Mk IIC(T) Bomber. To Burma.
LF203. Mk IIC(T) Bomber. To India.
LF207. Mk IIC Bomber.
LF284. Mk IIC(T) Bomber. To Burma.
LF295, 296, 322. Mk IIC Bomber.
LF325. Mk IIC(T). To Burma.
LF331, 333. Mk IIC Fighter.
LF342. Mk IIC Bomber. Conv to IIB Bomber. Sold Portugal.
LF346. Mk IIC Bomber.
LF360. Mk IIC Bomber. Sold Portugal.
LF363. Mk IIC Fighter. BoB Flight.
LF366, 368. Mk IIC Bomber.
LF376, 378, 380, 382, 383, 386, 393, 395, 396. Fighter.
LF398. IIC Fighter. To 5415M.
LF403, 404, 421 Mk IIC Fighter.
LF422, 425 Mk IIC Bomber. Sold Portugal.
LF428. Mk IIC Bomber.
LF430, 458. Mk IV(T) RPs only. To Yugoslavia.
LF463. Mk IV(T) Bomber. To Russia.
LF464. Mk IV(T) RPs. To Yugoslavia.
LF469. Mk IV Bomber. To Burma.
LF470. Mk IV Bomber. To Russia.
LF477. Mk IIC Bomber. To Burma.
LF482, 497, 498, 507. Mk IV(T) RPs. To Yugoslavia.
LF514. Mk IIC Bomber. Sold Portugal.
LF532. Mk IIC Fighter.
LF534. Mk IIC Fighter. Sold Eire.
LF536, 541. Mk IIC Fighter. Sold Eire 115.
LF564, 565. Mk IIC Fighter. Sold Portugal.
LF566. Mk IIC Fighter. Sold Eire 117.
LF568, 570. Mk IIC Fighter. Sold Portugal.
LF577. Mk IIC Fighter. No arms A/A duties.
LF580. Mk IIC. No arms A/A duties. To 5402M.
LF586. Mk IIC Fighter. Sold Portugal.
LF587. Mk IIC Fighter. Sold Portugal.
LF588, 600. Mk IIC Fighter. No arms A/A duties.
LF620. Mk IIC Fighter. Sold Portugal.

LF623. Mk IIC. No arms A/A duties.
LF624. Mk IIC Fighter. Sold Eire 118.
LF626, 627, 628, 636. Mk IIC Fighter. No arms TT A/A duties.
LF643. Mk IIC(T). To Italy.
LF644, 658. Mk IIC Fighter.
LF674. Mk IIC Fighter. To 5418M.
LF680. Mk IIC. To maintenance.
LF685, 689. Mk IIC Fighter.
LF699. Mk IIC Fighter. To Portugal.
LF703, 705. Mk IIC Fighter.
LF706, 717. Mk IIC Fighter. Sold Portugal.
LF744. Mk IIC Fighter. To 5405M.
LF745. Mk IIC Fighter. To 5406M
LF754. Mk IIC Fighter. To 5419M.
LF755. Mk IIC Fighter. To 5149M.
LF757. Mk IIC No arms. Sold Portugal.
LF770. Mk IIC. To Eire 119.
LF772. Mk IIC Fighter. Sold Portugal.
MW336. Mk IIC. No arms.
MW339. Mk IIC. No arms.
MW340. Mk IIC. No arms. To 5463M.
MW341. Mk IIC Bomber. To 5311M.
MW354. Mk IIC Bomber. To 5321M.
MW359. Mk II No arms.
MW360, 361, 367. Mk IIC No arms.
MW368. Mk IIC Fighter.
MW373. Mk IIC Fighter. To Portugal.
PG428, 429. Mk IIC Fighter.
PG440. Mk IIC Fighter To Italy.
PG444. Mk IIC Fighter. To 5462M.
PG469. Mk IIC Bomber. To Met IIC.
PG472. Mk IIC Bomber.
PG476. Mk IIC Bomber. To 5422M.
PG488. Mk IIC Bomber. A/A duties.
PG497. Mk IIC Bomber. To 5417M.
PG498. Mk IIC Bomber. To 5421M.
PG512. Mk IIC Fighter.
PG514, 515. Mk IIC No guns.
PG517. Mk IIC Fighter. To 5407M.
PG521. Mk IIC Fighter. To Portugal.
PG529. Mk IIC Fighter. To 5408M.
PG535. Mk IIC Fighter. To Portugal.
PG537. Mk IIC Fighter.
PG538. Mk IIC Fighter. To Portugal.
PG541. Mk IIC Fighter. To 5430M.
PG543. Mk IIC Fighter. To Portugal.
PG546. Mk IIC No guns.
PG567, 568. Mk IIC Fighter.
PG570. Mk IIC Fighter.
PG571, 573, 593. Mk IIC Fighter.
PG597. Mk IIC Fighter No guns.
PG599. Mk IIC Fighter. To Portugal.
PG604. Mk IIC Fighter. To 5416M.
PG610. Mk IIC Fighter. To Portugal.

PZ735, 738. Mk IIC Fighter. To Portugal
PZ740. Mk IIC Fighter.
PZ745. Mk IIC Fighter. To Portugal.
PZ751. Mk IIC Fighter.
PZ758. Mk IIC Fighter No guns.
PZ759. Mk IIC Fighter. To Portugal.
PZ768, 769. Mk IIC No guns.
PZ796. Mk IIC Fighter. To Eire 120.
PZ803, 805, 806, 807, 808. Mk IIC(Met) No

guns.
PZ809. Mk IIC.
PZ811, 812, 814, 815, 816, 817, 818, 819, 820.
Mk IIC(Met) No guns.
PZ821, 823. Mk IIC.
PZ830. Mk IIC(T)Met No arms.
PZ861, 863. Mk IIC Fighter.
PZ865 Mk IIC Fighter. To G-AMAU. 'Last of
the Many'.

Hurricane II (Austin) 300 a/c built during 1941. Serials. AP516-550, 564-613, 629-648, 670-714, 732-781, 801-825, 849-898, 912-936.

AP516,517. Mk IIB. Performance trls B Down.
AP518,519,521,522,525,530,533,539. Mk IIB.
AP566. Mk IIB(T).
AP851,852. Mk II(T) Tac R. To ME.
AP856. Mk IIB(T). To ME.
AP883. Mk IIB(T).
AP888. Mk IIC(T). To ME.
AP889. Mk IIB(T). To India.

AP892. Mk IIB(T).
AP894. Mk IIB(T). To Burma.
AP896. Mk IIB Bomber.
AP916. Mk IIB(T) Bomber.
AP920. Mk IIC(T) Met. To NA.
AP925. Mk IIB(T). To ME.
AP929. Mk IIB(T). To India.
AP930. Mk IIB(T).

Hurricane X. Fourth production batch of 100 (Canada). Merlin 28. Serials. BW835-884. All to Russia or retained Canada.

Hurricane XI. Fifth production batch of 150. Merlin 28. Serials. BW885-BX134.BW962, BW973, BX115. Mk NFXI. Turbinlite.

Huricane XI and XII. Sixth production batch of 248. Merlin 28 (XI), Merlin 29 (XII). Serials. JS219-371, 374-468. 185 a/c 12 gun wing (XIIB and XXB). 63 a/c four cannon wing (XIIC).

JS253. Conv to Sea Hurricane XIIB. To NA.
JS290, 300. NFXIIC. Turbinlite.
JS310, 327, 328. NFXIIC. Conv to Sea Hurricane
XIIB. To NA.
JS330. NFXIIC.
JS334. Conv to Sea Hurricane XIIB. To NA.

JS335. NFXIIC.
JS336. Conv to Sea Hurricane XIIB. To NA.
JS347. NFXIIC. Turbinlite.
JS418. Mk XIIC(T). To Persia.
JS465. Mk XIIC(T). To Persia.

Hurricane IIA. Seventh production batch of 150 a/c. (Canada). Merlin 29. Serials. PJ660-695, 711-758, 779-813, 842-872. 12 gun wings. To Russia or retained in Canada.

PJ719, 745. Mk XIIA(T). Four cannon. To India

PJ847. Mk XIIA(T). Four cannon. To Burma.

Hurricane Mk V. Single prototype only NL255. Specified for ground attack duties. Cancelled.

'Mohlomi' – an early presentation Huricane IIC, BP352.

'Kenya Weekly News' – a presentation Hurricane IV, BP452.

'Swaziland II' – a late-series presentation Hurricane IV, HW660. Swaziland also contributed money for Typhoons.

'*Orissa VIII*' – *a late-series Hurricane IIC, KW922, with long range fuel tanks. Over 200 British fighters were subscribed by Indian states.*

'*British Prudence*' – *a late-series presentation Hurricane IIC, KW924, with long range fuel tanks.*

The last Hurricane, PZ865, at Dunsfold airfield in 1960.